A Systematic Based Learning (GBL) in Organizational Teams

Transform Performance Through Experiential Learning, Social Learning and Team Dynamics

By

Ken Thompson

with introduction by

Charles Jennings

January 2016

Revision: 1.35

A Systematic Guide to Game-Based Learning (GBL) in Organizational Teams

A Systematic Guide to Game-Based Learning (GBL) in Organizational Teams

A Systematic Guide to Game-Based Learning (GBL)

This book will help HR and Learning professionals who need clear guidance and case studies to support their own work as they exploit team-focused game-based learning. It provides a deep analysis and clear guidance to help practitioners develop effective social game-based learning solutions.

CHARLES JENNINGS, Co-founder of the 70:20:10 Institute

This text is one of the "bibles" for the merging discipline of gamification, serious games, and simulations. It should be prominently displayed upon your bookshelf. The Appendices alone are worth the price of the text.

MICHAEL SUTTON, Chief Gamification Officer at FUNIFICATION LLC and purveyor of sims and serious games within immersive learning environments.

This book is a great introduction to game-based learning for organizations and businesses. It is pitched at just the right level to give a sense of some of the issues associated with deploying these strategies in teams. I like the balance of practical advice and theoretical background.

CARLTON REEVE, Founder of Play with Learning Ltd

Some writers 'show off' their knowledge/skills. Ken does not do this as his knowledge/skills in these areas are first class and the style/content speak for themselves.

ALAN ANDERSON, Vice Principal, Cambridge Flexible Learning

While there are many books on game design and adult learning, I would place this short book at the top of the list for anyone interested in game-based learning (GBL).

DR. ROSS WIRTH, Professor and online course developer

A Systematic Guide to Game-Based Learning (GBL) in Organizational Teams

Ken Thompson has done a fantastic job of collating everything you want to know about Game Based Learning and then some. The clarity of message and layout is as impressive as the bucket-load of additional elements provided in the Appendices. Read this once to get a solid overview and a second time to uncover a wealth of insights to propel your own activities forward.

SIMON PHILLIPS, The Change Maker Group, Transformation, OD and Personal Development

Ken Thompson is one of the world's leading authorities on Game-based learning (GBL). Here he lays out the keys to using GBL in organizations to rapidly build new skills and competitiveness.

JEAN GOMES, Co-author of the New York Times bestseller, The Way We're Working Isn't Working

I love this book and found it extremely helpful. It's a wonderful reference full of expert advice. I learned and marked several things I want to implement.

JOYCE OSLAND, Executive Director, Global Leadership Advancement Center, San Jose State University

The way Ken manages to fit so much into a relatively short book is impressive.... No waffle, just straight to the point. I found myself asking questions throughout which were promptly addressed. Some very interesting ideas and concepts that I was able to relate to real life scenarios. A very clear and concise guide to GBL.

CHRISTOPHER HALLETT, Chartered Manager, UK Banking Sector

Ken Thompson's short volume provides a sound introduction and valuable blueprint for running Game-Based Learning for Organizational Teams.

JULIE VALENTINE, Events Commissioner at UNICOM Seminars

A Systematic Guide to Game-Based Learning (GBL) in Organizational Teams

Thanks so much for lending me Ken Thompson's 'A systematic guide to game-based learning in organisational teams', it's a fantastic read!

I particularly enjoyed the simple, direct approach; it does just enough to outline the merits and options around GBL but doesn't labour the point. Rather it assumes people agree and want to get on with implementing. The implementation guidance is equally direct, helping you to focus in on the type of game best suited to your challenge and equally what won't work and why.

The book moves logically through planning, designing, testing and of course executing a GBL, all backed up with further reading links and a very comprehensive appendix. All in all, it does exactly what is says on the tin, it's a systematic guide to GBL, a great read and a great reference, highly recommended, oh and of course I love that many of the examples have an aviation theme which I can readily relate to and also translate well to NATS situations.

ADAM WILLIAMS, Learning Technologies Consultant, NATS

A Systematic Guide to Game-Based Learning (GBL) in Organizational Teams

Contents

A Systematic Guide to Game-Based Learning (GBL) in Organizational Teams

A Systematic Guide to Game-Based Learning (GBL) in Organizational Teams

A Systematic Guide to Game-Based Learning (GBL) in Organizational Teams

About the Author

The book is authored by Ken Thompson who is an expert practitioner, author and speaker on collaboration, high performing teams, change management and game-based learning.

Ken has written several books and his work has featured in major publications including *The Guardian Newspaper*, *Wired Magazine*, *The Huffington Post* and *The Henry Ford Magazine*.

Ken has also spoken at a number of international events including TEDx, the Institute for Healthcare Improvement (IHI) and NASA conferences.

Ken is the author of "The Systematic Guides" series which includes:

A Systematic Guide to High Performing Teams (HPTs), Ken Thompson, December 2015

A Systematic Guide to Business Acumen and Leadership using Dilemmas, Ken Thompson, February 2016

A Systematic Guide to Change Management, Ken Thompson, July 2016

A Systematic Guide to Collaboration and Competition in Organizations, Ken Thompson, March 2017

All books are available on Amazon and make ideal delegate briefing notes for participants in game-based learning sessions by providing the underpinning theory and supporting best practice on each key topic.

Foreword by Charles Jennings

Organizations across the world are evolving their approaches to workforce development so they can improve their competitiveness and ensure their people are equipped to work to their maximum ability.

One of the major changes being brought about through these new approaches is the move from viewing learning as a formal and structured set of activities that are separate from work to one that views learning as a dynamic and interactive process that is part of the daily workflow.

Game-based learning and team-based learning are both fundamental parts of this change process.

This extremely practical book explains how to develop and exploit team-centric game-based learning. The initial parts of this book will help inform senior managers who are looking to improve the ways they can sustainably support the development of workforce capability in their organisations.

The book will also help line managers who want to explore and use tested new approaches to build team effectiveness.

In particular, this book will help HR and Learning professionals who need clear guidance and case studies to support their own work as they exploit team-focused game-based learning.

It provides a deep analysis and clear guidance to help practitioners develop effective social game-based learning solutions.

This publication is also extremely timely. Developments in mobile and social technologies, together with the consumerisation of the workplace are bringing about major changes in the way we live and the way we work. They are also opening up opportunities to change the way we learn. The contents of the following pages show the reader how to go about these changes.

Charles Jennings

Director, Internet Time Alliance
Co-founder of the 70:20:10 Institute

Winchester January 2016

EXECUTIVE SUMMARY

The guide offers a comprehensive and pragmatic framework for achieving transformational learning and behavior change in groups of leaders/managers using Game-Based Learning (GBL) in organizations of all shapes and sizes.

Chapter 1 explains exactly what GBL is and why there is so much interest in it.

Game-Based Learning means using games primarily for learning rather than fun, achievement and competition. I say "primarily for learning" because to be effective, even games for learning will be drudgery unless they are also fun, create a sense of achievement, and have an element of competition.

I suggest in the guide that there are at least 7 key ingredients which should be present in an engaging and useful team business game. These are Narrative, Dilemmas, Scorecards, Time Pressure, Surprises, Collaboration and Competition.

Business games themselves can be categorised in several ways, but I find it simplest to think of them in three categories:

- Business Acumen Games
- Specialist Skill Games
- Interpersonal Skill Games

Three key aspects of GBL are the use of simulations, experiential learning (learning by doing) and social/informal learning (learning by sharing experiences with others). Another important influence on GBL is "Gamification" which refers to gaming techniques such as points, levels and badges. GBL is another name for Gamified Learning, a key subset of Gamification.

A Systematic Guide to Game-Based Learning (GBL) in Organizational Teams

Chapter 2 reviews key quantitative and qualitative evidence for the effectiveness of GBL and includes 3 recent GBL case studies.

Research supporting the key elements of GBL suggests that:

- *Gamification* can make people engage more, learn/retain more, and change behavior better.
- *Business Simulation* is more effective than case studies, best if it uses real data, improves learnings, and requires skilled facilitation.
- *Informal/Social Learning* accounts for 80-95% of all operationally relevant learning.

The guide includes 3 GBL Case Studies which the author was involved in:
- Spar Wars (A fully Custom GBL Solution)
- Glasgow City College, Retail Fashion Game (An Off-the-Shelf GBL Solution)
- Twining's B2C Simulation (A Customized Off-the-Shelf GBL Solution)

The main benefits which players report after experiencing GBL include:
- Virtual Experience
- Social Learning
- Resolving Dilemmas
- Change and Pressure (Agility)
- Confidence and Ambition

Chapter 3 explains why the focus of the guide is specifically business learning games used in teams.

The reason the guide is focused on teams rather than on individuals is to facilitate the powerful social aspect of learning which is simply not possible when an individual is playing a simulation game alone. A further focus of this guide is on learning specifically aimed at leaders and managers (including prospective leaders and managers) and not non-management specialists or generalists.

Chapter 4 proposes a systematic approach to GBL with 4 stages that are each described in detail in chapters 5 – 8:

- GBL Planning
- GBL Design
- GBL Testing
- GBL Execution

The main steps in GBL Planning are:

- The Target Learning Community and its Top Challenges
- High-Level Learning Objectives (Topic-Team-Touch)
- Learning Strategy (for target capabilities)
- The GBL Business Case

The main steps in GBL Design are:

- Project Roles
- Model Design
- Solution Provision: Buy vs. Build vs. Customise
- Information Design
- Supports (Stage Directions and Props)
- GBL Design Options
- Game Psychology

A Systematic Guide to Game-Based Learning (GBL) in Organizational Teams

The main steps in GBL Testing are:

- Design Concept Test
- Business Rule Test
- Scenario Test
- Landing Test
- Facilitator Test
- Pilot Test

Chapter 8 also introduces a pragmatic execution model which cycles round the key steps as shown in the figure below:

Finally, the guide also offers readers a **free** *GBL Business Case Calculator* (written in Microsoft Excel), which navigates step by step through the tricky process of GBL benefits and costs estimation. The guide concludes with a comprehensive set of Appendices containing a wealth of relevant supporting material.

Chapter 1: What exactly is Game-Based Learning?

Game-Based Learning means using games primarily for learning rather than fun, achievement and competition. I say "primarily for learning" because to be effective, even games for learning will be drudgery unless they are also fun, create a sense of achievement, and have an element of competition.

GBL can be used for purely educational purposes at universities and schools or purely for business purposes in organisations. GBL can also be participated in as an individual or as part of a team. <u>The focus of this guide is specifically on business learning games played in teams.</u>

Business games themselves can be categorised in a number of ways, but it is simplest to think of them in three main categories:

- **Business Acumen Games** – where you are learning about a particular type of business or about business in general
- **Specialist Skill Games** – where you are developing specialist skills such as Risk Management or Project Management
- **Interpersonal Skill Games** – where you are enhancing interpersonal skills such as Influencing or Negotiation

Business games may be a mixture of two or even three of these categories, however, effective games will have a clear primary focus or else will suffer from a lack of cohesion and be confusing and unsatisfying for the participants. This is a key risk for the designer of business games – the management of focus and the control of complexity, an important topic that we will discuss later on in the guide.

1.1 Why all the interest in GBL?

There are a number of reasons including:

- The rise of and hype around the term "Gamification[1]" [1] (the use of gaming techniques for non-gaming purposes). GBL is really just another name for Gamified Learning, a key subset of Gamification. The Global Gamification market was $421.3 million in 2013 but is forecast to grow to $5.50 billion by 2018, at a staggering CAGR of 67.2%. [2]
- The predominance of "apps" on mobile phones and tablets means people now want to learn by playing games.
- The increasing popularity of experiential learning (learning by doing) and social learning (learning by discussing) as the preferred way of acquiring new skills is fuelling the interest in GBL.
- If you search for "simulator" on your iPhone or iPad app store you will be overwhelmed by an abundance of all types of simulators, including flight, spaceship, train, car, and business simulators. This is reflected in the level of interest in simulation games for learning increasing from 14% in 2013 to 31% in 2014. [3]

1. Appendix Q provides a short Review of popular Gamification Techniques.

1.2 What do we actually mean by the term 'game'?

Jane McGonigal, in her book "Reality is Broken" [4], proposes the following four "defining characteristics" of a game:

1. A Goal
2. Rules
3. A Feedback System
4. Voluntary Participation

Jane illustrates how these 4 components apply to various different types of games, such as Golf, Scrabble, and Tetris and controversially suggests that the "ability to win" may not be a defining characteristic of a game.

1.3 What makes a 'good' game?

There is a lot of debate by game designers and players about 'what makes a game a good game' [8]. Although this dialogue is mostly about games for entertainment, I believe we can build on their valuable insights to identify 'what makes a team-based business game engaging and useful'? By 'useful' in this context I mean *valuable as a learning development tool for individuals and teams*.

I would suggest there are at least 7 key ingredients which should be present in an engaging and useful team business game. These are *Narrative, Dilemmas, Scorecards, Time Pressure, Surprises, Collaboration* and *Competition*.

1.   Narrative

The narrative of the game must be relevant to the participants. For example, if the participants are the leadership team of a cruise ship then a game involving running a retail fashion clothing business is unlikely to engage them fully. The game does not have to be modelled on the participant's business, although sometimes this is required, but it does need to be relevant and meaningful to the intended players. A key aspect of the narrative is the 'Briefing' that the participants are given about the game. If the briefing is done well (message, mood and messenger) it will inspire the players and also trigger their imagination to collaborate with the game designer by helpfully filling in any 'realism gaps'.

2.   *Dilemmas*

In most discussions about games there is a consensus that a good game involves 'meaningful' decisions. This means decisions which are non-trivial and to which there may be no obvious best answer - in other words 'dilemmas'. Such decisions allow participants to agonise over their choices which also greatly enriches the conversations within the team. (I discuss the role of *dilemma-based design* as a technique for ensuring a strongly focused central game narrative in Chapter 6). A good game will only have the absolute minimum number of decisions needed to achieve its goals - this is the design concept of 'Requisite Complexity'.

3.   *Scorecards*

It almost goes without saying that the players of a game need to be able to see at any point, in some attractive and clear visual representation, how they are currently doing in the game. Game 'scorecards' should show not just the progress against the ultimate game goals but also the status of any critical indicators which are the 'drivers' of the final scores. A good game will employ the important principles of 'Information Design' to ensure the visuals are actually useful and not just an exercise in 'shock and awe.

4.   Time Pressure

An important element of a business game is making decisions under pressure. This makes it more real-world and also this stress is important in facilitating the rapid evolution of team dynamics. One of the most common forms of pressure and stress is impending deadlines which must be met. It is also important that all teams can see exactly how much time they have left at any point on a 'common clock' over which there can be no arguments about how long is left or wasteful negotiations for time extensions?

5.   Surprises

In the real world things change all the time and change is a key ingredient of a good team business game. The game 'surprises' need to be both nice and nasty and both relevant and irrelevant ('red herrings'). The surprises can be embedded in the game or they can be external to the game or best of all - a synchronized combination of both. An important related aspect of well-designed game surprises is 'multiple-media/modes'. By this I mean the game effectively blends multiple forms of media to engage the players. Media/Modes include the computer, hard copy, audio, video, props and human interventions (senior business people, facilitators, subject matter experts and even actors).

6.   Collaboration

In a good game there should be more work involved in addressing the challenges than can be handled by a single individual within the time constraints. This forces the participants to divide up the work in some way. This 'division of labour' and roles is a great a catalyst for both helpful and unhelpful team dynamics!

7.   *Competition*

There is a lot of competition in the real-world as we are all naturally competitive (despite what we might claim). A good game has the added spice of competition to make sure participants take it seriously and try to do their very best. It is important however not to let the competitive side of the game get out of hand or this will be at the expense of the learning. At the end of a good game players should have learned AND enjoyed themselves. In an overly competitive game participants may miss much of the important learning insights in the mad frenzy of trying to win at all costs!

1.4 Gamification, Simulations and Serious Games

At this introductory stage it may also be helpful to try to differentiate between these three similar terms, which frequently cause confusion. Linda King [5] writes an article in her blog that succinctly suggests the difference between them:

Gamification is all about applying game elements (the 'DNA' of games) to non-game activities to make them more compelling. Gamification leverages 'game mechanics' such as points, levels, badges and achievements.

Simulations* are real and immersive games which offer an experiential educational experience. Simulations place people in a risk-free environment which supports their engagement in an authentic experience which contextually demonstrates benefits and consequences.

Serious Games use traditional game craft techniques (for example, video game technology and strategy) around serious concepts such as business, education, environmental, or social issues.

I believe it is important to recognise the huge debt we in the Learning and Development field owe the aviation world for its many years pioneering in the whole field of flight simulation. Appendix E summarises the history of aviation flight simulation and what we can learn from it in business.

1.5 Experiential, Social and other learning models

Finally, still in the context of our introduction, it is important to mention some of the key theories of how people learn and the terminologies associated with them.

Carlton Reeve has written an excellent series of five articles in Play with Learning [6]. He compares and contrasts the five main theories of learning. These are *Behaviorism, Cognitivism, Constructivist, Experientialism,* and *Social Learning.* I have summarised the five theories in Appendix F of this guide, however, it is worth briefly expanding here on the most recent one – Social Learning.

Have you ever asked yourself "How much of the essential knowledge which I need for my job was acquired through some kind of formal learning?" The answers are surprising; research by my colleague, *Jay Cross*, and published in his book "Informal Learning," [7] suggests that typical answers to this question are only between 5 and 15%.

So what is the significance of this little statistic?

Firstly, it means that you are probably acquiring 85-95% of your essential knowledge through what Jay would call "Informal Learning" techniques. In simple terms there are 3 main Informal Learning Techniques:

1. Trying things out and learning by making mistakes
2. Conversations with your colleagues and bosses
3. Self-motivated reading and research

You should recognise that these often forgotten and discounted historical techniques are actually *still the most important ones for effective learning* and need to be part of any serious approach to team-based GBL.

Secondly Jay's 5-15% statistic means that other people in your work network probably already know what you need to know. It follows that if only 5-15% of "essential knowledge" learning is formal then any mixed experience group probably already collectively knows 85-95% of what is needed for any task that group might be asked to do. This underscores the value of team-based learning along with colleagues.

1.6 Virtual Team Games: Any Time? Any Place?

The games I describe in this book often run in *'Same Time/Same Place'* mode with the participants all in the same place at the same time.

However, many organizations today either run fully virtual (non-co-located) teams or find it impractical to bring groups of 20-30 individuals into the one place at the one time for at least half a day. With careful planning and the right technological support (using technologies such as *webex, gotomeeting, join.me, adobe connect* and even *skype*) it is completely possible to run these team games successfully in other modes which support virtual team working.

A Systematic Guide to Game-Based Learning (GBL) in Organizational Teams

The easiest mode after 'Same Time/Same Place' is *'Same Time/Any Place by Team'* where each of the teams is in a different place.

In this mode you can use virtual technologies to ensure there is some kind of real-time audio/video communication between the teams at the different locations at the beginning, end of each round and end of game. This allows the team members to get a sense of inter-team competition and to share learning with the other teams.

Somewhat more challenging but still entirely feasible is *'Same Time/Any Place by Individual'* where every one of the individuals is in a different place.

In this mode you need to be able to create a number of virtual breakout rooms, each one private to a team. These breakout rooms should support shared team desktops which allow all team members to see/edit their game screens and updates. There also needs to be a real time team audio/messaging facility so virtual team members can privately communicate with each other. As with the previous mode there also needs to be communication with all the players at the beginning, between rounds and at the end. It is also very helpful if facilitators can eavesdrop/intervene with the different teams.

Going beyond these 3 modes into *'Any Time/Any Place'* (sometimes referred to as 'Martini-mode') is rather difficult for team games unless they are exclusively focussed on 'Topic' (see chapter 5.2 for more on this) as it is very challenging to create any authentic sense of team dynamics when all players are operating exclusively asynchronously via email and messaging!

Many thanks to Karen Foundling for sharing her experiences and insights from running team exercises and games with virtual participants.

Further Reading

1. Gamification 2020: What is the future of Gamification, *Gartner Research*, 2012

2. Gamification Market Worldwide Market Forecasts and Analysis (2013 - 2018), *marketsandmarkets.com*, 2013

3. Learning & Development Technology Report, Impact *Instruction Group*, 2013

4. Reality is Broken, *Jane McGonigal*, Vintage Digital, 2011

5. Understanding the difference between Gamification, Simulations and Serious Games, *Linda King*, 2012

6. Play with Learning, *Carlton Reeve*, http://playwithlearning.com/

7. Informal Learning, *Jay Cross*, Pfeiffer, 2006

8. What makes a Game, *Keith Burgun and Commenters*, http://www. gamasutra.com, 2012

Chapter 2: How effective is Game-Based Learning?

2.1 Research

The most effective GBL seems to blend 3 important components - Gamification, Business Simulation and Informal/Social Learning. I will try to summarize some the key research findings on the effectiveness of each of these disciplines:

Gamification can make people engage more [2], learn/retain more [3], and change behavior better [4].

Business Simulation is more effective than case studies [5], best if it uses real data [5], improves learnings [6], and requires skilled facilitation [7].

Informal/Social Learning accounts for 80-95% of all operationally relevant learning [1].

OK, but what is the evidence for the 3 disciplines working together as GBL?

Jessica Trybus, a Game-based Learning Guru and Director at Carnegie Mellon University, has conducted research [8] into 3 different approaches to learning. Jessica evaluated passive training methods such as classroom lectures and e-learning, hands-on training such as apprenticeship programs and game-based learning across 8 potential benefits:

A Systematic Guide to Game-Based Learning (GBL) in Organizational Teams

1. Cost-effectiveness
2. Low physical risk/liability
3. Standardization of assessments allowing comparisons
4. High Engagement
5. Learning pace tailorable to individual
6. Immediacy of feedback in response to mistakes
7. Ease of transfer of individual learning to work place
8. Learner Engagement

The research concluded that passive training delivered the first 3 benefits, hands-on training delivered the last 5 benefits but **game-based learning delivered all 8 benefits!**

In other words, well designed game-based learning can combine the benefits of both passive training and hands-on training.

Gartner Research, a major influencer concerning whether and when specific new technologies actually make business sense for major organizations, [9] sums it up very nicely by advising their clients in a major report that:

"GBL can significantly accelerate the transfer and application of knowledge. Enterprises should leverage the scalability and immersive characteristics of games to accelerate the time to competency and the depth of competence".

Finally, in Appendix R, I summarise current research about what makes gamified learning effective both neurologically and psychologically and, based on this, propose a simple **"Cognitive Framework for Effective GBL"** which can be used as a checklist by GBL designers.

2.2 Case Studies

Now that we have looked at the quantitative I will summarise the results from just three of many case studies to give you some *qualitative* insights into the benefits of GBL. More details and further case studies can be found at http://dashboardsimulations.com/category/case-studies/

Before I do this, however, it is interesting to note that most GBL is delivered in the context of Leadership and Management Development Programmes. *Deloitte* recently published research [10] suggesting that a well-led/well-managed enterprise can be up to 70% more valuable than a poorly managed one - all else being equal.
This gives some idea of the potential prize for companies who are able to use GBL to sustainably improve the leadership and management skills in their organisations.

Spar Wars (A fully Custom GBL Solution)

SPAR is a major convenience store group located across UK, Ireland and Europe. The retailer puts a strong emphasis on providing excellent customer service, choice, and value, to allow a more convenient shopping experience closer to home. They also feel strongly about supporting local suppliers and the local community.

As a result of a detailed discussion with senior leaders from *The Henderson Group*, who operate the SPAR Franchise for Northern Ireland, it was established that their store managers needed to spend more time developing their people to improve staff retention, and also to focus more on customer service to retain the most loyal customers.

They decided to commission a custom GBL solution (*Spar
Wars*) that would allow participants to experience
managing a convenience store over a half day, but
representing four trading months, and allowing them to:

- Manage store service levels across a range of
  business aspects via visual KPIs
- Maximise store financial performance each month
  and for the total trading period
- Use good judgement in moving resources from one
  part of the store to another

Sam Davidson, Group Human Resources Director,
Henderson's, who sponsored the project and provided
subject matter expertise made the following observations
about the simulation:

*"We have developed a powerful business simulation that
allows our managers to run one of our convenience stores
for 4 months in a single day. The pressurised, realistic and
highly competitive nature of the game brings a unique
dimension to the learning. We are expecting to gain
significantly higher benefits and engagement from this
game than other forms of training."*

Glasgow City College, Retail Fashion Game (An Off-the-Shelf GBL Solution)

The requirement was for a fashion specific retail simulation for students that would give them a practical insight into the real decisions and dilemmas that buyers and merchandisers actually encounter within the dynamic retail fashion sector.

There was also a requirement for a team-based simulation, to allow students to experience working in teams to discover what type of team players they are, and how well they work together under pressure.

The *Catwalk* Retail Fashion Simulation allows teams to run a major designer fashion brand in a national market over 4 seasons. For a team to succeed they need to be running a profitable, fashionable and socially responsible business. The simulation is conducted using a highly structured approach that blends gamification and informal/social learning. In this instance it was played with 4 competing teams with 6 students in each team (with one team made up of just lecturers to add a bit of spark to the competitive edge).

Key aspects of the simulation included:

- The importance of product design and "product outfit families" to maximise customer basket size
- Correctly positioning your different product brands in the market in terms of pricing, image and material/production costs
- Managing offshore manufacturing in a manner consistent with good Corporate Social Responsibility (CSR)

- Anticipating and responding well to both supply-side changes and sales-side trends, including competitor activity.

Maureen Houston, Retail Course Leader at Glasgow City College, who introduced and monitored the game, made the following observations:

"It makes what I have been teaching in class really come to life. The simulation is also really useful for students as it teaches them to appreciate suppliers' roles and the importance of good suppliers. I think the competition aspect really engages the students, and I liked the added touch of a prize for the winner. I could definitely see the simulation being used over the course of a whole module, in which students could study a season one week and debrief the next week."

Twining's B2C Simulation (A Customized Off-the-Shelf GBL Solution)

Twining's, based in Andover, Hampshire, is world famous for its distinctive teas and malt drinks. Twining's operates internationally within the Associated British Foods (ABF) Group. Each year Twining's runs a week-long Leadership Development Programme for high-potential managers.

A full day of this programme is dedicated to *Consume*, an immersive Team-Based Business Simulation game, where the participants form executive teams to compete intensively in running Twining's Country businesses for a full 3-year period, marketing three types of premium teas against a realistic set of competitors' market shares.

A Systematic Guide to Game-Based Learning (GBL) in Organizational Teams

The business simulation requires the teams to engage with the central dilemmas of such a venture including:

- Price Elasticity (The impact of Price on Demand)
- Product Mix & changing Consumer Preferences
- Profitability _versus_ Market Share Growth
- Value Chain Investment _versus_ Organisational Health Investment

Simon Brocket, International HR Director at Twining's, who sponsored the simulation and provided subject matter expertise for the business simulation, made these observations after the game had been run with multiple teams of managers over a 3-year period:

"Realistic simulation is a powerful though often overlooked and underutilised approach to building capability. The business simulation we developed gives people an experience that calls for them to develop and deploy competitive strategy. The learning people derive from the experience is very powerful, and because it is theirs the transfer to the workplace is so much easier. We have been able to use the same business simulation over and over again with different groups within the company so the Return on Investment has been exceptionally good for us."

2.3 Benefits

When I interview game participants or business sponsors after GBL events the benefits they report (directly and indirectly) consistently fall into 5 clear categories:

1.   *Virtual Experience*

This is the classic flight simulator learning model where participants get to try out 'dangerous things' in a safe and forgiving environment with no adverse business consequences. [For more detail on the history of aviation flight simulation and what the learning games industry can learn from it please see Appendix E].

'Virtual Experience' is not only the important decision-making which participants can practice but also the scenarios they encounter. Also the major and minor unexpected 'shocks' which they have either brought on themselves or which have been pre-programmed into the simulation game beyond the participants control.

A number of participants have spoken with me 6-12 months after GBL events and reported that 'things which happened in the sim actually happened afterwards in the real world'. This should not be such a surprise as a good game designer will base some of the in-game shocks on actual events which happened in the past to give the game realism and on the assumption that history often repeats itself!

2.   *Social Learning*

Social Learning is learning from others through conversation and sharing. In the context of GBL this means learning from fellow game participants, subject matter experts, facilitators and senior business participants. It is a common lament of larger companies that 'we don't know what we know'. A well-designed social GBL game is one of the most effective ways for organizations to disseminate and spread knowledge, experience and best practice between colleagues. [For more on Social/Informal learning please see section 1.5, 8.8 and Appendix F].

3.   *Resolving Dilemmas*

Any well designed GBL event will present the participants with dilemmas. These can come in many forms and include business dilemmas, leadership and team dilemmas. [see section 6.2]. Simulation games should reflect the real world in that there are rarely enough resources (such as money, people, machinery and stock) to achieve everything you would ideally like to achieve.

Hard choices have to be made in the light of the participants understanding of their organizational priorities, targets and values. A well facilitated team game can allow participants the space to 'play with dilemmas' creatively in a much more relaxed way than would ever be possible in their real jobs. In so doing they may discover some new solutions and approaches they never even considered before.

4.   *Change and Pressure (Agility)*

As well as having to address dilemmas and scarcities a GBL event should also model the real world situation that things are always changing unexpectedly and that there is always a time pressure factor. This is very the essence of 'agility' – the ability to handle unexpected change well and in a timely manner.

A Systematic Guide to Game-Based Learning (GBL)
in Organizational Teams

One of the most important leadership skills is to be able to determine which deadlines can be moved and which ones cannot. For example, the discipline of submitting your team's results on time (or being penalised) helps people understand the non-negotiability of certain financial reporting deadlines particularly in big organisations where there is an extensive review and consolidation process which, to work, requires all its inputs competed and submitted to a strict deadline.

5.   Confidence and Ambition

Finally, a common theme reported by game participants 3-6 months have a game event is that they feel more confident and are taking on bigger responsibilities in their jobs/roles. When I ask the question 'why' a common response is that the game they played was very challenging but yet they still succeeded (for example, running a flour mill or a country business unit in the face of challenging trading and market conditions)!

The participants in such as game often feel they, and their colleagues, really achieved something worthwhile. There is interesting learning here for GBL designers around 'requisite difficulty'. A game needs to be difficult enough to be a real challenge and for the 'jury to be out' until near the end as to whether they will succeed or not. But it must not be so difficult that participants feel they failed in the end as most (but not all) people find it hard to take positive learning from this kind of experience.

In a sense this final benefit is really a consequence of the other 4 benefits but I encounter it so frequently I think it is worth listing it here separately.

Game Dimensions and Learning Modes

Finally, in closing on the GBL benefits topic, there are two further important observations about the benefits possible from GBL:

Game Dimensions

Each of the 5 benefits listed could be realized in any or all of the 3 'Game Dimensions' – topic, team or touch [for more on Game Dimensions please see section 5.2].

So, for example, a participant might gain 'Virtual Experience' of the specific skills involved in being a leader on a cruise ship plus the team dynamics of this plus insight into how they personally reacted under pressure in this situation.

Game Learning Modes

Each of the 5 benefits could also be realised through any or all of the 3 'Learning Modes'– planned, shared and serendipitous [for more on Learning Modes please see Appendix M].

This means that participants have effectively 3 bites at the cherry of learning in a GBL! They might learn something because they were looking to learn it (planned), and/or because somebody else shared it (shared) and/or because it just came up out of the blue (serendipitous).

Further Reading

1. Jay Cross, Informal Learning, Pfeiffer, November 2006
[Multiple References, especially Appendix. B]

2. Peng & Heeter, "Darfur Game" Study, 2010

3. Traci Sitzmann, University of Colorado, Video Game Players
Study, 2010

4. Luchini, Norris & Soloway, Maths Game User Research,
2004

5. Kenworthy and Wong, Management Simulator and Game
Study, 2005

6. Andrew Feinstein, Food Service Industry Simulation Study,
2009

7. Samuel Certo, The Role of the Experiential Exercise
Instructor, 1976

8. Game-Based Learning: What it is, Why it Works, and Where
it's Going, Jessica Trybus, New Media Institute, 2014

9. Key Reasons why you should consider learning by gaming
Strategy, Gartner Research, 2006

10. The Leadership Premium: How Companies Win the
Confidence of Investors, Deloitte, 2013

Chapter 3: Focus of this guide

As I mentioned in the first chapter, the focus of this guide is specifically business learning games used in teams.

The reason the guide is focused on teams rather than on individuals is to facilitate the powerful social aspect of learning which is simply not possible when an individual is playing a simulation game alone. We discussed the high value of the social learning impact in the first chapter.

Such sessions can be also virtualized, with different teams all playing in different locations via central video link communications, while still maintaining most of the social learning benefits.

You might also ask "Is it possible to create a social learning effect if the individuals are playing as a team but all in different locations?" The answer is "yes," but to a lesser degree provided you can find a way to connect the individuals electronically using messaging or virtual meeting technologies *during and after* the game interaction.

This becomes even more difficult if the individuals are participating in the simulation at different times, as you must then rely only on after-the-fact engagement for any social learning effect.

A further focus of this guide is on learning specifically aimed at leaders and managers (including prospective leaders and managers) and not non-management specialists or generalists. This is primarily because of the huge benefits to be gained from improving the management and leadership of organisations (reference the *Deloitte* research in chapter 2).

This is not to say that GBL does not have a massive role to play in practitioner development, but it is a large area and I do not want to dilute to focus of this guide. For example, there are huge benefits to be gained in areas such as medical simulation tools for doctors and surgeons promoted by organisations such as *The Center for Medical Simulation* [1]. There are also great examples of using simulations to teach *mission critical individual skills* in areas as diverse as Mining, Construction, Agriculture, Health & Safety and Emergency Services [2].

Note: For practical reasons to provide space for learning (experiential and social) within the time constraints where participants can be together, the games I describe in this book are based on the structure of a fixed number of rounds of pre-determined lengths.

Further Reading

1. The Center for Medical Simulation,
   https://harvardmedsim.org/
2. ForgeFX Custom 3D Job-Training Simulations,
   http://forgefx.com/industries/

Chapter 4: Structure of a Game-Based Learning Project

A GBL project can be thought of as having 4 main stages that proceed in a broadly sequential order, but with iteration backwards and forwards as required:

- Planning
- Design
- Testing
- Execution

Each of these four stages can be broken down further into a number of steps:

4.1 GBL Planning

This covers the initial discussion about using a GBL Solution through feasibility and ending with the authorization and funding to proceed.

The main steps in GBL Planning are:

- The Target Learning Community and its Top Challenges
- High-Level Learning Objectives (*Topic-Team-Touch*)
- Learning Strategy (for target capabilities)
- The GBL Business Case

4.2 GBL Design

This covers the design of the simulation plus any supporting materials and the decision whether to build and/or buy.

The main steps in GBL Design are:

- Project Roles
- Model Design
- Solution Provision: Buy vs. Build vs. Customise
- Information Design
- Supports (Stage Directions and Props)
- GBL Design Options
- Game Psychology

4.3 GBL Testing

This covers all the different types of tests that will be needed along the way, from initial concept through to a full test with a live audience.

The main steps in GBL Testing are:

- Design Concept Test
- Business Rule Test
- Scenario Test
- Landing Test
- Facilitator Test
- Pilot Test

4.4 GBL Execution

This covers all aspects of running a successful GBL event on the day.

The main steps in GBL Execution are:

- Pre-Event
- Team Briefing
- Mental Models/Personal Objectives
- Team Game Plans
- Team Discussions
- Team Decisions
- Team Results Analysis
- Team Learning Review
- Team Results Review
- End of Simulation Team Review
- End of Simulation Individual Review

In the next four chapters I will describe each of these stages and steps in detail.

Chapter 5: GBL Planning

5.1 The Target Learning Community and its Top Challenges

A key first step in planning for GBL is to identify the target community, where the organisation needs them to be collectively in terms of their performance to deliver its future business results, and what the current "capability gap" looks like.

One way to do this is to consolidate the performance and skills of the top performers in the group to create an *ideal profile*. Sometimes, however, top performers achieve their results at some cost to others in the organization in terms of their personal style, so it is helpful to also include what top performers may be <u>missing</u> in this ideal profile.

For example:

"We want all the Sales Manager group to be able to hit $10M annual revenue targets and delight their customers *(the good bits)* whilst also taking care of their team members and *peers (the missing bits)*. To do this they will need to get much better at forecasting and listening to their customers and their team members *(the key capabilities)*".

Once you have built up and validated the ideal performer profile you can then assess other performers from the community against it. A pragmatic way to do this is to assess some poor performers, some average performers and some good performers. The capabilities all three types are missing are obviously top priority.

5.2 High-Level Learning Objectives (Topic-Team-Touch)

Initial "Top Challenge" statements tend to be somewhat high-level - they must then be progressively broken down into specifics and measurables.

If you are considering a team-based GBL approach, then it is useful to consider defining the learning objectives across three specific domains of potential learning **Topic-Team-Touch** (aka Skills-Social-Style):

- **Topic** is the specific topic the GBL would need to address such as Business Acumen or Influencing Skills.

- **Team** is everything to do with what could be learned by participating in a GBL team and could include things like team roles, decision-making and conflict resolution. I have carried out research into the difference between top performing and other teams *playing business simulations*, revealing a number of important lessons on what really constitutes high-performing teams. (See Appendix B for a summary)

- **Touch** is everything to do with the learning around how individuals might show up in the GBL event, including their style in engaging with their colleagues and how they interact with GBL facilitators, business sponsors, and subject matter experts.

So our example GBL learning objectives might start to look like this:

Topic: Business Development with Sales & Revenue Forecasting.

Team: Better understanding of what makes a High Performing Sales Team work and what gets in the way.

Touch: Spotting and challenging assumptions, reacting quicker to address potential issues, communicating more effectively with senior people.

Appendix O discusses how you can use Team GBL to develop 7 other key management skill areas which I call 'Talent'.

Appendix C offers a checklist of 28 specific capability areas that Team-based GBL could address. Obviously you cannot address all 28 areas in a single GBL intervention – you need to choose priorities!

5.3 Learning Strategy (for target capabilities)

Best Practice versus Best Experience

It is now useful to think a bit more about the nature of the missing capabilities in the target community.

There are really two types of capability – *Best Practice and Best Experience.*

Best practice is the documented and agreed way of doing things. Best practices generally have core aspects which transcend industries and companies and other aspects which are industry / sector / organization specific. However, the key thing is that Best Practice is generally *explicit and documented* and you may already have your own best practice documented for your organization.

Best experience is the (usually) undocumented way top performers achieve excellent results. It will often be situational. For example, how they deal with dilemmas (more later under "Dilemma-Based Design" in the GBL Design Chapter). An example of Dilemma Resolution would be negotiating a compromise which satisfies a customer and which manufacturing can live with in terms of capacity and lead times. The key thing about Best Experience is that it is generally *implicit and undocumented*. It is also personal – it resides in the top performers.

If the missing capability is Best Practice, then you need somebody on your team who is considered a Subject Matter Expert and can guide the GBL design appropriately. If the missing capability is Best Experience, then you need somebody on your team who is considered a Top Performer and can guide your GBL design appropriately. *It is important that you don't get a Subject Matter Expert when you need Best Experience and that you don't get a Top Performer when you need Best Practice!*

It is generally more difficult to get a Top Performer on your team for the obvious reasons. Also you will need to work very closely with them during GBL design to make sure that the conversations which arise from the GBL will actually facilitate the surfacing and sharing of their experience.

In many cases the required knowledge for the GBL will be a mix of some Best Practice plus some Best Experience and often the GBL element will not address all of what is required, with the rest being addressed by a mix of blended learning. Again, it is important to control the scope and complexity of the GBL (see more under GBL Design).

Target Community Engagement

You also need to think about how you plan to engage and transform the target learning community via the GBL. There are 3 main strategies – *Shift, Catch-up* and *Top-Up* - each shown in the diagram overleaf with its normal distribution curve.

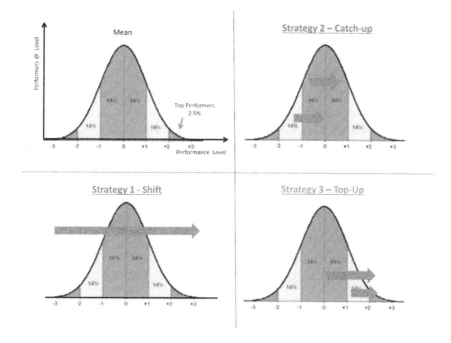

There is also a fourth strategy, the *Cull* Strategy made popular by the likes of *Jack Welch* at GE, where each year you remove the bottom 10% of the community. Apparently, this explains the origin of the term "decimate" – a barbaric Roman army practice wherein to quell a mutiny, you executed 10% of the soldiers. It is certainly a way to improve the mean performance, and might be used in conjunction with one of the other 3 strategies, but is certainly not one any far-sighted organization would rely on in isolation.

Strategy 1 – Shift

This is the most common approach where you attempt to move the needle on *every member* of the community to some degree. This can be a very good approach if you have to address issues around compliance and minimum standards, and may lend itself also to technologies such as e-learning. However, this "one size fits all" approach can be impersonal and may be more challenging to apply effectively where a significant behavior change is required.

Strategy 2 – Catch-up

In this case you concentrate on bringing both the seriously under-performing and the below average performers *up to the mean* performance level. Like the previous strategy this can be effective for compliance issues but for deeper issues it will need a more personal touch, which might, for example, include one-to-one coaching and mentoring. It's also a tricky one to manage from a motivational point of view if it becomes seen as a remedial performance class. This strategy may also go somewhat against current research by organisations such as Gallup [1] indicating that performance improvement is best achieved by building on strengths rather than repairing weaknesses!

Strategy 3 – Top-up

This is often the forgotten strategy. Instead of bringing the community or a subset of it up to some common standard of performance you decide to study and partner with your top performers to see if you can reduce the *spread* between their performance and the average performance. We have already discussed the key questions you need to find the answers to in terms of what it is that your top performers do differently than the rest (their secret sauce). Strategy 3 generally fits well with a GBL solution.

5.4 The GBL Business Case

Before you commit to any significant expenditure on a GBL project you should prepare a GBL Business Case. I will outline here a simple and robust 6-step process for doing this, which is supported by an Excel-based GBL Business Case Calculator [2] that will guide you step-by-step through all the steps. *(You can request a free copy by emailing me – contact details at the end of this guide)*.

There are 3 steps involved in estimating the financial benefits resulting from a learning intervention such as GBL with an individual Leader or Manager.

Step 1 - Identify Leader's Potential Financial Impact
First look at the potential universe of financial value that the leader engages with and the extent to which their leadership can impact upon it.

Step 2 - Assess Key Leader Skill Levels, Targets and Weightings
Secondly identify the key skills of the leader, their current levels and the target improvements in these levels expected from the specific intervention you are planning. You can also weight each of these skills in terms of relative importance to the financial measures. The figure overleaf (taken from the spreadsheet) is a *Spider Diagram* showing the gap between target and current skill levels for a leader or specific category of leaders across 5 different priority capability areas.

Before & After Leadership Skill Levels

————Current Leader Skill Level (See Table 1)

————Target Level after Leadership Devel (See Table 1)

Step 3 - Estimate Financial Benefits of Leadership Development Intervention
Next, calculate the financial impact based on the percentage of the "Perfect Skillset" which the intervention is expected to deliver.

There are now 3 more steps to extend your analysis to the whole community and to include benefit phasing and, of course, cost.

Step 4 - Aggregate the Benefits to the whole target leader community
You need to identify the benefits of the intervention for each member of a group of leaders, then aggregate them. Alternatively, if the group is too big to deal with on an individual basis you can do the calculations on a single typical

member of the group and multiply this by the total number in the group. The best practical solution is often to split the group up into a small number of performance bands (e.g. High, Middle, and Low) and make an assessment for each band which you can then multiply by the number of people in each band to get your total benefits estimate.

Step 5 - Consider the phasing of the benefits
This will give you the benefits of the intervention per annum. You can then decide how these benefits would be realized over a normal investment appraisal period (e.g. 3 years). You might, for example, conclude that only 50% of these benefits might accrue in the first year followed by 80% in year 2 and 100% in year 3.

Step 6 - Do the cost-benefits analysis
Now that you have the total timed benefits of the investment, it is very easy to compare this with the costs of the intervention over the same period to work out the return on investment. In Appendix H, I summarize the half a dozen different calculations which can be used to support Business Cases.

Further Reading

1. Now Discover your Strengths, *Marcus Buckingham*, Gallup Press, 2013
2. A free GBL Business Case Calculator, 2014 http://www.bioteams.com/2014/06/28/a_free_leadership.html

Chapter 6: GBL Design

6.1 GBL Project Roles

There are a number of key Project Roles that should be established before you start a GBL Design project:

Project Sponsor
This is the senior businessperson who sponsors the costs of the GBL project in expectation of the benefits.

Project Manager
Reports to the Project Sponsor and is responsible for the day-to-day management of the GBL Project.

Lead Subject Matter Expert (SMEs)
Responsible for ensuring the GBL project correctly interprets Best Practice and/or Best experience. Where they do not know the answer themselves, they will liaise with other SMEs, but they will be responsible for ensuring it is not GBL design by committee!

End User Representative(s)
Responsible for testing the GBL with a view to how it will "land" with the intended audience. (See GBL Testing Chapter for more details).

Lead Designer
Responsible for building, modifying, and configuring the GBL to satisfy the learning requirement. Works very closely with the Lead SME and Lead Facilitator.

Lead Facilitator

Responsible for ensuring that the learning outcomes are delivered by the GBL event. They will often be supported by a number of other facilitators and they will work very closely with the Lead SME and Lead Designer. (See GBL Testing Chapter for more details)

6.2 GBL Model Design

One of the biggest challenges for a GBL designer is how to work out which aspects of a topic will bring the most value to a community of learners. A technique called *Dilemma-based Design (DbD)* [1] is particularly helpful if the learning topic is one that has grey areas such as influencing others or managing a business or team or department. DbD should build on the discovery work done during GBL Planning, and particularly the High-Level Learning Objectives.

Dilemma-based design suggests that in any job or team or organization there will always be a small number of dilemmas which bring most of the challenges, and that good performance is largely down to how well practitioners can resolve or "square" these dilemmas.

I would sharply contrast dilemma resolution with decision-making: decision-making involves right and wrong answers, but in the case of dilemmas there is always some pain or compromise or trade-off involved, <u>no matter which option gets picked</u>.

To develop this idea a bit further a key element of a game is that the players should not have enough resources to do everything they want to do. *Scarcity or shortage* will force the players to make priority trade-offs and will generate great conversations that are rich with learning potential.
There are two main types of dilemma: *Leadership dilemmas* and *Business dilemmas*. Leadership dilemmas are nearly always present in a similar form, whereas Business dilemmas depend entirely on the nature of the role or organisation.

A good example of a Leadership dilemma is working as part of a collective team. You may have very strong views on something but sometimes you may have to run with a collective view of the team, which is different from your own view. So you need to resolve the dilemma of whether you push a decision hard based on your opinion, or you back off based on your judgement that the team knows best, or that it is not important enough to have a big team argument over! This dilemma is present whether you are a team member or the team leader.

A good example of a Business dilemma is Product Mix. Let's imagine the market is starting to tell you they are less attracted to your old faithful Product A and want more of your new Product B. However, it is not ideal for you to just switch, as you have lots of Product A stock and production facilities, and Product A may be much more profitable than Product B with all its investment costs already fully written off. You have a dilemma!

You can either react to the market by switching towards Product B or you can try to lead the market by trying to change customer preferences back towards Product A, via marketing and/or discounting. Which one will be effective depends on the interplay of a number of things, one of which is the degree to which your company is perceived to be a market leader or market follower in the product area.

The figure below identifies five common Leadership dilemmas and five common Business dilemmas that I most frequently encounter in my discussions with top practitioners and subject matter experts in organisations.

For a more detailed exploration of each of the ten dilemmas please watch my short *YouTube* video [4] or checkout my book 'A Systematic Guide to Business Acumen and Leadership Using Dilemmas'.

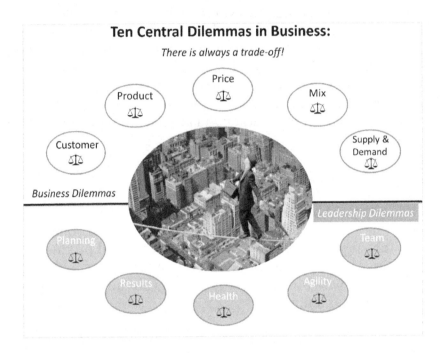

As a broad guideline, I would suggest you should aim to construct team business simulation games by combining 2-3 leadership dilemmas with 2-3 business dilemmas.

A Systematic Guide to Game-Based Learning (GBL) in Organizational Teams

I know from experience that if I design a game with fewer dilemmas then it will probably not be sufficiently realistic or challenging. On the other hand, if I have more dilemmas, say I went mad and built in all 10 dilemmas, then the game would be far too complex. It would also lack cohesion – a bit like a film designed by committee with some romance, cowboys, and science fiction. [Actually, come to think of it, just like the film "Cowboys versus Aliens" with *Daniel Craig*].

So when you are talking with a practitioner or Subject Matter Expert, don't just ask them what they do or even what decisions they have to make. Ask them what dilemmas and trade-offs keep them awake at night. If you can build the learning around this you are much more likely to create a more engaging, valuable, and enjoyable experience for them.

So the successful outcome of this stage is to extend the High-Level Learning Objectives with about half a dozen key dilemmas with a concrete example of each describing the "horns of the dilemma", the various complications, the consequences of the various choices and an "optimum" decision.

Appendix D identifies 15 principles for Business Game Design for Team-based Learning, which is useful in conjunction with DbD as it offers a number of practical design tips.

Appendix K proposes 12 rules for good simulation design based on hard experience.

6.3 GBL Provision: Buy vs. Build vs. Customize

Now that you have identified the target community, Learning Objectives, and key dilemmas, you need to decide how you will obtain the GBL solution. There are 3 alternatives:

Off-The Shelf (OTS) GBL

This is best when you have some flexibility in your requirements and gives you the choice of a large number of potential solutions, both web and desktop based. In this case you need to plan for a procurement project where you shortlist and select a suitable supplier. The Retail Fashion Game described in section 2.2 is an example of an Off-the-Shelf GBL Solution.

Custom GBL

This is best where you have specific requirements which cannot easily be met by a standard GBL solution. It will be more expensive, so it only really makes sense if you have a large target community (100+ learners) who will benefit from the GBL and therefore reduce cost per head. There will also be a lead time (normally at least 3 months) to allow for the design, development, and testing which you would need to allow for in your plans and schedules. Because it is being designed from scratch it will probably also require ongoing Subject Matter Expert (or Top Performer) input.

In this case you need to plan for a design and development project where you progressively review different versions of the developing solution against your learning requirements. You should try to obtain a fixed price quotation against your requirements to mitigate against scope and budget creep. The

Spar Wars simulation described in section 2.2 is an example of a fully Custom GBL Solution.

Customised OTS GBL

This is a middle ground where 80% of your requirements can be met by an Off-The-Shelf Solution, which then requires some customization to meet the remaining 20%. As with the Custom GBL you should try to obtain a fixed price quotation against your requirements to guard against scope/budget creep. Twining's B2C Simulation described in section 2.2 is an example of a Customised Off-the-Shelf GBL Solution.

There are two very important considerations *irrespective* of which GBL provision option you decide to go for:

- You are not just selecting a technology partner - you also need someone who can credibly facilitate and deliver the GBL solution and/or offer you a train-the-trainer service.

- You will need a written project plan with a well-defined and agreed schedule of milestones, with clear responsibilities and review points. Appendix I offers a High-Level Template Plan for Custom GBL Development which you can tweak as required.

6.4 Information Design

Please note that if you go down the route of custom GBL development you will need to have somebody on your design team who is familiar with the principles of Information Design and how important this is for GBL screens or dashboards.

As a brief introduction to this important and poorly understood topic I have extracted 7 key principles of Information Design from *Stephen Few's* excellent book, "Core Design Principles for Displaying Quantitative Information", which you should consult for a full understanding.

A common mistake in the design of GBL screens is to try to make them pretty or cute. For example, dashboards that actually look like aeroplane dashboards are probably great for flight simulators but not a business simulation game used by leaders and managers in airline or aerospace companies!

What seems cool in a demo but not well thought-out from an Information Design perspective will soon cause needless frustration and confusion in GBL teams once the pressure is on.

Failures in GBL Information Design may be spotted during the Landing Test described in 7.4 – but only provided representative end users are given adequate time to play with the game. A mere GBL demo will not reveal this type of problem. This is also a very costly place for such failures to occur, as they may mandate a rewrite of the GBL and threaten project deadlines and budgets.

7 Principles of Good Information Design

1.   Display neither more nor less than what is relevant to your message.

2.   Do not include visual differences in a graph that do not correspond to actual differences in the data.

3.   Use the lengths or 2-D locations of objects to encode quantitative values in graphs.

4.   Differences in the visual properties that represent values should accurately correspond to the actual differences in the values they represent.

5.   Do not visually connect values that are discrete, thereby suggesting a relationship that does not exist in the data.

6.   Make the information that is most important to your message more visually salient in a graph than information that is less important.

7.   Augment people's short-term memory, by combining multiple facts into a single visual pattern that can be stored as a chunk of memory, and by presenting all the information they need to compare within eye span.

6.5 GBL Supports

<u>GBL Documentation</u>

The main types of documents required to support GBL solutions are:

Delegate Pre-Reading Material

This is information which will be given to the participants or teams in advance of the simulation, and will contain items such as key background briefing material, the starting position, simulation definitions, rules and anything else participants need to reference during the simulation (and which is not available as on-screen help). Generally, you should restrict this to only information which is absolutely essential, as too much too soon can quickly overwhelm participants.

Simulation Updates

Usually between each round of a simulation things change (e.g. Competitor Activity, Raw Materials Price Rises and Internal Company Issues). Teams may be notified of these changes directly by the simulation or by the facilitators handing out information pages at the appropriate time. I prefer the latter, as it is more like the real world.

These updates have three purposes. Firstly, to see how well the participants react to change. Secondly, to test their skills in *Information Filtering*. Thirdly, to see how committed the teams are to their chosen strategies. Therefore, the information should be a mix of severity, urgency, and relevance.

There is interesting research within the field of Behavioral Economics [2] (and briefly summarized in Appendix G) about various irrational biases we are all subject to. One of these is known as the *Availability Bias* where we irrationally treat the latest piece of information (or its absence) as the most important thing on our agenda. A bit like why we always answer the phone, no matter what else we are doing. Therefore, good GBL design should include some 'Red Herrings.'

A useful check on your simulation updates is to grade them using the 'Three Spans Model'[3]:

- *Span of Control* – effects things which I can control
- *Span of Influence* – effects things which I cannot control but I can influence
- *Span of Concern* – effects things which I neither control nor influence

To make Information Filtering more challenging, simply turn up the volume of information so team members do not have time to read everything individually. This also forces teams to consider whether they are effectively dividing their labour (i.e. role allocation).

Simulation User Guide/Facilitation Manual

This documentation helps the facilitators by giving them the significance of the information being given out to the team participants. Facilitators should also be given clear instructions on their roles (See Appendix A) and on how the end of round and end of simulation discussions are to be conducted. A very practical tip is for facilitators to each be responsible for documenting at least one per GBL event (with the answer of course), which then can be collated and used at subsequent GBL events.

GBL Stage Directions and Props

Well thought-out stage directions and props can make a simulation more realistic, more intense, more multi-dimensional, or more conflictive, for the purpose of accentuating specific learning objectives.

Examples of stage directions and props include:

- *Role Plays,* for example, forcing teams to interview a facilitator to test listening skills

- *Facilitator Review/Scoring* of Team Responses, for example, to test teamwork and team communications

- *Control of Simulation PIN Codes*, for example, forcing teams to seek approval

- *Managing Director in the Game*, for example, seeing how well teams communicate with a very senior business person

- *Changes in Timing*, for example, progressively knocking 5-10 minutes from each simulation round duration, to force teams to work differently or smarter

- *Rotating team leadership,* for example, to let team leadership experience be shared

- *Moving participants between teams,* for example, to see how well teams incorporate new members

- *Giving participants private instructions*, for example, "Be Argumentative this round" to see how teams deal with conflict

- *Sound Effects*, for example, end of round sounds which create a sense of urgency (or panic) in the other teams

- *Dressing the room*, for example, product images on the walls to help teams get into to the context deeper and faster

- *Specific props*, for example, leaving information on team tables but not drawing attention to it to challenge assumption-making

- *Inter-team Communications*, for example, to see how well teams can collaborate

- *Communications Protocols,* for example, teams may only talk with other teams whilst seated in designated communication zones to make communications more business-like or challenging

- *Hats and T-shirts*, for example, to differentiate the teams for competitiveness or to highlight the individual currently playing a key role in a team such as rotating team leader

- *Prizes*, for example, best performing team or most improved team or the team who demonstrated the best learning insights

However, these things must be used carefully and in moderation, as we must remember they are only valuable if

they enhance the learning outcomes and *not just as fun things
in themselves.*

6.6 GBL Design Options

There are a number of design options you should consider
within your GBL Design. Here are two very important ones:

In Game Competition Design

There are two main ways teams can compete within a GBL
session – within the game or outside the game.

'Competing within the game' means that each team's decisions
impact the other teams' decisions within the game. So, for
example, if it is a Business Acumen game then each team could
be a business competitor of the other teams and so if one team
gains market share then the other teams must lose it. In
technical terms this means that there is one overall simulation,
which all the teams are playing within.

'Competing outside the game' means that each team is
effectively playing the same simulation (against the computer)
but in total isolation from the other teams. In this case
competition can only be in terms of comparing the results each
team is achieving each round. Played like this the teams are
not competitors in the game, and in the business acumen
example all teams could be growing market share against their
computer-based competitors.

Which one should you choose?

There are pros and cons for both options.

'Competing outside the game' scenarios mean that you can better control the learning experience. For example, you can have the computer-based competitors increase their prices in round 3 automatically, whereas in the other scenario it is totally down to the other teams when or if this happens. Also if you need to simulate very complex business rules, then 'competing outside the game' is probably the better option as you don't have to worry so much about the composite effect of the rules plus all the other team moves.

'Competing within the game' scenarios can, however, be very exciting and engaging with your competitors all in the same room. However, the learning experience is less controllable and if one of the teams makes extreme (or silly) moves then this will impact the learning experience of all the other teams. Also in the 'competing within the game' option you need to keep the game quite simple as it can become difficult for players and the facilitator to actually make sense of what is actually happening in the game at any moment.

Fixed versus Dynamic Teams

In a fixed team model the GBL teams remain static over the full game, whereas in a dynamic scenario the teams are changed every round.

Which one should you choose?

Like competition design, there are pros and cons for both options.

In a fixed team GBL you get the chance to really develop the dynamics between the members of the team and a strong sense of team and loyalty can develop. The downside is that a team can become locked into a certain dynamic that may be hard to shift.

In a dynamic team GBL you reform the teams each round. You can do this in lots of ways for example in round 1 team A is all the people with birthdays January to March, round 2 it is all the people with surnames starting A- F, and in round 3 it is all the people from Sales.

Dynamic Grouping creates one very powerful option – the ability for individuals to take their team scores with them each round, so that by the end of the game each individual has a unique personal score. If that is what you want to do, then dynamic grouping is a great way to use a team game to achieve it.

Dynamic grouping can also be useful if you want to focus on how well teams form, but it is not so useful for exploring mature team dynamics.

Finally, there is a hybrid of the two options where you exchange or transfer some people between teams in some rounds. This can be useful if you want to focus on how well mature teams take on new members.

6.7 Game Psychology

To close this chapter, here are a couple of important observations on game design psychology learned from hard experience:

"It is always better to be on the ground wishing you were in the air than in the air wishing you were on the ground."

Old Pilot Quote

Always leave them wanting more

It is always better to be one round short and have the participants wanting more than one round too many and having the participants wanting it over. In my experience 3 or 4 rounds of a game is usually enough for anyone.

Remember the Easy-Hard-Easy Sandwich

The first round should always be the simplest and the most generous in terms of time allocation to allow the participants to absorb the new information and game mechanics.

Likewise, the final round should generally not be the most difficult, as you don't want people to finish feeling like losers. This leaves the middle one or two rounds for really challenging and stretching the participants – they can be the hardest ones.

If you do it like this you give the participants time to absorb the game, really challenge them, and then leave them feeling that they have had a demanding but basically successful learning experience.

It's fine for GBL teams to feel they are winners so long as none of them feel they are losers!

Further Reading

1. Dilemma-based Design: Managing focus and complexity in business games, *Ken Thompson*, http://dashboardsimulations.com/dilemma-based-design-focus-reduce-complexity-serious-business-games/
2. Predictably Irrational: The Hidden Forces That Shape Our Decisions, *Dan Ariely*, Harper Perennial, 2010
3. Principle-Centred Leadership, *Stephen R. Covey*, Rosetta Books, 2009
4. Ten Dilemmas: A short video intro to dilemma-based design for Business Simulation Games Video, *Ken Thompson*, http://dashboardsimulations.com/ten-dilemmas-short-video-intro-dilemma-based-design-business-simulation-games/

Chapter 7: GBL Testing

There are six main types of tests which may be required before you can let loose your GBL solution on your target audience:

7.1 Design Concept Test

This is to verify that the design concept, as shown with a screenshot or mock-up, meets the learning objectives. It normally involves the Project Sponsor and Lead Subject Matter Expert (SME) and usually happens during the design phase. It is still required even if it is an Off-The-Shelf GBL Solution as these are often generic simulations that can be employed in different ways.

An important aspect of this test is whether the main simulation decisions screen(s) are appropriate for and useable by the intended target audience. A key challenge here is *Requisite Complexity* [1] – too simple and the participants won't be engaged by it or will need to reference addition information. Too complex and they will be confused and take too long a time to get comfortable.

7.2 Business Rule Test

This normally involves the Lead Subject Matter Expert (SME) or Top Performer and its purpose is to verify that the GBL solution has correctly interpreted any business rules. This is not just the rules but also the magnitude of effects. For example, how much impact on demand should a 10% reduction in pricing actually have? Will it increase demand by 15%, 10%, 5% or not at all?

The Lead SME needs to check that whatever values are used are reasonable but not necessarily exact. Remember when you see adverts for games on the TV and it sometimes says, *"Some sequences have been shortened!"* This also applies to simulations where it is sometimes necessary to exaggerate the effect of decisions to make sure the consequences are clearly visible in perhaps a shorter timeframe than would normally be the case.

Appendix J proposes a practical modular blueprint for designing any simulation in a way that allows its rules to be verified and tested objectively.

7.3 Scenario Test

This also usually involves the Lead Subject Matter Expert (SME) and its purpose is to verify that the scenarios used in the GBL solution are appropriate and realistic and won't fail any "sanity checks" with the live in-house company audience.

By "scenario" we mean two things. Firstly, the starting position and opening values of any key metrics such as organizational KPIs. Secondly the impact of the automatic background changes in the settings of the simulation each round, and the way they are described in the supporting briefing papers that are given to the participants or displayed on the screen. Sometimes there is a pressure to combine the Business Rule Test and the Scenario Test. This is not a great idea, as they are both testing very different things.

7.4 Landing Test

This is where a *90%-ready* version of the simulation is tested
with colleagues who aim to represent the Target Audience
(End User Representatives). The first objective is to check
whether it is too easy or too difficult, meaning that new aspects
might need to be added or some aspects removed. The second
objective is to check whether it is a good engaging learning
experience in line with the key learning objectives. The final
objective is to catch all the little things that would distract
from a top-quality learning experience, such as wrong or
awkward terminology and unrealistic or inaccurate briefing
materials.

It is important to go through the whole simulation if possible
on this test, however, the most critical thing is that a good 30-
60 minutes is left at the end for the "guinea pigs" to give their
honest feedback on whether the GBL is fit for purpose. This
provides the vital directions on how it needs to be improved,
changed, or simplified, before running with the live target
audience.

7.5 Facilitator Test

This test is where the facilitators play at least some of the GBL
solution as participants and then discuss and agree how they
will facilitate it.

A practical approach is for the facilitators to play the first
round(s) of the simulation as participants and then try to move
more into observing/facilitating in the latter rounds.

This test can be combined with the Landing Test, if required,
where the facilitators stay on after the "guinea pigs" have left.

This test is therefore also a Train-the-*Trainer* session for the facilitators.

7.6 Pilot Test

The Pilot test is the first live run of the simulation in full, with complete briefing notes for the intended audience, and with the facilitators playing their roles in full.

This test should confirm that the GBL solution will achieve the required learning objectives with the target community. If it does not, then you are back to the drawing board as you have missed something important!

The Pilot Test will also inevitably identify a number of small snags in the software and the documentation and provides the opportunity to correct these annoyances before the GBL solution goes into general rollout.

Further Reading

1. The law of requisite variety and team agility, Ken Thompson, http://www.bioteams.com/2007/10/22/the_law_of.html

Chapter 8: GBL Execution

The illustration below summarizes the main stages in a GBL event. The nine steps shown would typically be cycled round 3 or 4 times. At this point you would conduct the End of Simulation Reviews (Team and Individual). Prior to this you will need to do some key Pre-Event work, and this is where we will start. Appendix I contains a sample agenda for a half-day game with typical sequence and timings.

<u>Please note</u> the model illustrated above has been very carefully designed and tested to exploit best practice in both *Experiential Learning* and *Social/Informal Learning* in a team/group setting (see Appendices M, N and O).

8.1 Pre-Event

I am assuming you have already done all the event planning, venue communications, and delegate communications, and you have arrived at the venue in good time to prepare for the arrival of the GBL participants.

There are 3 key things you will need to take care of before they arrive:

1. *Set up the room (s)*

You will need to make sure the room is in an appropriate layout for team-based GBLs. You don't want everybody round a large table *United Nations* style. You want them in team tables with a bit of space between them to stop the teams overhearing and distracting each other.

Teams should generally have 4-8 participants – ideally 6. Smaller than this and it will lack a realistic team dynamic. Bigger than this then some team members may be somewhat passive if there is not enough for them to do. If your budget allows for team breakout rooms, this can be very helpful too, in helping participants quickly get into role.

2. *Set up and test all hardware and software*

You need a computer at the front of the room projected on a big screen (important that the projector has hi-resolution – many old ones are good enough for *PowerPoint* but may not have enough resolution to do your simulation screen justice), plus a computer on every team table.
To enable all team members to see their screens the team computers should have at least 16-inch screens. It is even better if you can connect a large external screen or TV to each

team computer via the HDMI slots. If the simulation runs over the internet, you should check the connections are good in all corners of the room and not just at the front.

You may find my *4 Golden Rules of Technical Set-up* useful here:

RULE 1: <u>Never</u> assume anything that previously worked still works.

RULE 2: <u>Always</u> assume power adapter problems – bring spare extension cables.

RULE 3: <u>Always</u> allow 15 minutes just to set up the screen projector properly.

RULE 4: <u>Never</u> try to fix a technical issue in front of a group – give them a 5-minute coffee break!

3. *Organise all the delegate briefing materials*

GBL events ironically tend to require a lot of printed paper handouts. Make sure the different types of papers are sorted into a convenient order for handing out to delegates at the appropriate time. There is nothing more embarrassing than not actually being able to find the handout you have just described in detail.

8.2 GBL Team Briefing

Step 1: The Team Briefing ensures that the overall GBL solution is put into a meaningful business context and imbued with a sense of seriousness that "this is not just a game". This step can be supported by off-sim business briefing materials which contextualize the game. A vital aspect of this step is also to set the game objectives and determine exactly how success will be measured ("targets"). Sometimes from a learning viewpoint it is useful to make these vague, incomplete, or ambiguous, to give teams the opportunity to clarify them verbally (or not).

It is also usually helpful at this stage to give the participants a demonstration of the simulation and then immediately allow them to play with it for 15 minutes in a short Familiarisation Round. This will help them get comfortable with the dynamics of the screen without the pressure of being live with the clock ticking. The simulation should be reset at the end of the familiarisation round.

8.3 Mental Models/Personal Objectives

Step 2: Mental Models are one of the most critical steps in setting up a game for success. A critical element of these GBL events is to challenge participants' mental models about what it takes to be a high performer in a specific business or leadership area.

You just can't do this unless you first take the time to "surface" participants' mental models [1] (a key experiential learning technique). This is best done by inviting the participants to draw out simple "cause and effect" models linking the decisions in the game to the results they think will be produced. If you neglect this step there is a serious risk that the participants will try to "game" the simulation by guessing its underpinning rules. Playing a game like this, just to win, is unfortunately of limited value in terms of learning and behavior change. You want the participants to do what they would do in the real world based on what they believe ("their mental models"), not what they think they need to do to win the game.

A Systematic Guide to Game-Based Learning (GBL)
in Organizational Teams

The figure below is a fragment of a mental model used by participants in an Automotive Commercial Acumen Simulation. It shows, for example, that Materials Cost Reduction has the *primary* effect of reducing Variable Costs plus a *secondary* (delayed and unintended) effect of reducing demand and actually increasing costs if it goes too far and damages product quality and results in warranty claims.

What is your Mental Model of the Business?

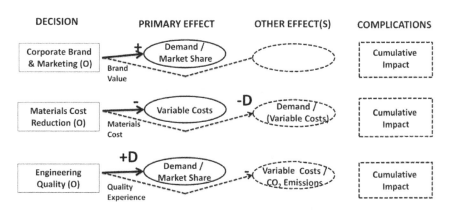

Personal Learning Objectives

The other key aspect of this step is Personal Learning Objectives. This is the "I" in the "I-We-I" learning sandwich where individuals should be invited to reflect on what they would like to learn from the GBL event before they start playing it as a team. This should cover the 3 domains of learning (Topic-Team-Touch) and the 3 modes of learning (Planned-Shared-Serendipitous).

The three types of Social Learning (Planned-Shared-Serendipitous) are defined and explained in Appendix L.

8.4 Team Game Plans

Step 3: Team Game Plans is where each team playing the game looks at their goals and targets and then, based on their shared mental models, comes up with their strategy or game plan for excelling. It is important that the teams are encouraged to think of the simulation as running a real business area or project and not just a game, as this will help them interpret any ambiguities (which there always are) in their objectives and targets in a more powerful way. Typically, I give a team the following guidance in terms of what they should cover in terms of summarising their Game Plan on a one-page flip chart displayed on the wall:

1. **R**oles
How will we divide up the team responsibilities?
2. **A**greements (Ground Rules)
How will we deal with each other as colleagues and team members?
3. **P**rocesses/Practices
What are the 2-3 most important team processes/practices will we put in place and follow?
4. **P**riorities
How will we decide what is most important, particularly in dilemmas or under pressure? [2]
5. **O**rganizational Values
What values are the most important to us as a team?
6. **R**esults
What specific results must we achieve as our minimum team performance level?
7. **T**argets
What is our 'stretch' target, our ambition to exceed our minimum performance level?

'RAPPORT' is a useful mnemonic for the 7 key elements of a Team Game Plan as it means: '*A close and harmonious relationship in which the groups concerned understand each other's feelings or ideas and communicate well.*' Source: OXFORD DICTIONARY.

8.5 Team Discussions

Step 4: Once the teams have established their game plans they need to decide on decisions for the particular game round, which make sense in the light of their stated strategies. This is where facilitation is crucial as somebody needs to ensure that discussions are inclusive, comprehensive and that decisions are based on evidence, not just player's gut-feel or prior knowledge. The facilitator also needs to shut down low-value conversations (e.g. how do we win this game) and amplify high-value conversations (e.g. what would we do in our real business in this situation).

A full checklist of GBL Facilitator Responsibilities is included in Appendix A

8.6 Team Decisions

Step 5: Team Decisions is where the teams enter their decisions into the simulation and see what results they produce. It is important to record the decisions and their rationale (in the team game book) to enable the participants and facilitators to conduct any necessary post-mortems later. It's amazing how different team members' recollections of the decisions they made can be if nobody has kept a hard copy record!

A hard copy of the decisions is also essential in the event of some kind of computer glitch or power failure and a team has to re-enter their decisions from the start of the game to recover their current position.

8.7 Team Results Analysis

Step 6: Team Results Analysis is where the team review the
results they just achieved for the round, and see where this
leaves them in terms of their targets and what changes in
priority or strategy they may have to consider in the next
round. Well-designed games provide a dashboard of indicators
based on the principles of the Balanced Scorecard [3] which
offer a mix of lagging indicators (e.g. financial results) and
leading indicators (e.g. organizational health) that give early
warnings of likely future business results.

8.8 Team Learning Review

Step 7: Learning Review is where the team and its participants
capture learning whilst it is still fresh. Team learning can be
captured by placing stick-it notes on a central *Learning Board*
each round, which capture fresh insights (typically things done
well, badly, and surprises). Learning Boards also allow teams
to learn from the insight gained by other teams and this should
be encouraged as a very effective Informal Learning technique.

Individual insights should be recorded each round as this is
ultimately how the game should conclude with individuals, not
teams, making commitments around behavior changes and
KPIs impacted back in the business. (see under End of
Simulation Review).

A Systematic Guide to Game-Based Learning (GBL) in Organizational Teams

It is important to remind ourselves that there are always 3 domains of potential learning in any team game:

- The Subject Area (e.g., Change Management or Running a B2C Business)
- Team Dynamics (how we are working as a team)
- Individual Dynamics (how I am working as an individual)

At the end of each round, teams should be given 10-15 minutes to discuss and reflect on a small number of key questions typically:

- How are we working as a team – what might we improve?
- How are we doing in the simulation – what might we change?
- How closely are we following our team game plan – does this need to be revised?

Each team should then be given the opportunity to very briefly share a summary of their insights (1-minute maximum) with the other teams to maximise the social learning effect.

In addition, another useful device I often employ at the end of the first round is to have the teams self-assess against the '7 *mistakes teams make under pressure*' (see overleaf) and then share this with their facilitator/other teams.

A Systematic Guide to Game-Based Learning (GBL) in Organizational Teams

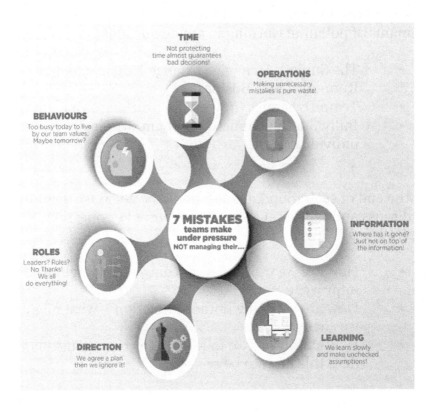

8.9 Team Results Review

Step 8: Team Results Review is where each team's performance is compared using a running *Leader Board* which records the key performance measures through which the different teams will be judged. This should summarise the game dashboards and contain a mix of financial and non-financial indicators. A concise Leader Board skilfully and sensitively shared and revealed can create great competitive tension and team motivation.

This provides an essential balance to the sense of collaboration in collective learning. In our experience the Leader Board should always be the last thing in the round (and at the end of the game) as it then sets the teams up nicely for starting the next round. Also, if a Leader Board is done too early or is too dominant in a round, it makes teams reluctant to share their learning as the sense of competing and winning can take over.

8.10 End of Simulation Team Review

This is where you should give teams the opportunity to take some time to reflect on their overall GBL learning experience. One way to do this is to give each team 20 minutes to prepare a short team presentation covering:

- How did we do? What worked well for us?
- What would we do differently if we did it again?
- What new insights have we gained?

8.11 End of Simulation Individual Review

Now we have finished the teamwork we need to allow some
time for the individuals to reflect on their personal learning.
This is the final aspect of what I called the *I-We-I* learning
sandwich where we ask the delegates as individuals to

1. *Record* the new insights they personally have gained
2. *Connect* this to their behaviors in their job roles
3. *Commit* to what impact this will have on their personal
   KPIs

I can't stress enough the importance of this final step in
landing the benefits that all the investment in the GBL was
designed to produce. Some organisations also schedule a post-
event debrief meeting or conference call, e.g. in 3 months'
time, where the participants can share their considered
reflections and more importantly talk about the concrete
difference it is making in their jobs.

Further Reading

1. Poor Mental Models fail teams before they even
   start? Ken Thompson,
   http://www.bioteams.com/2010/10/05/poor_ment
   al_models.html
2. The Discipline of Market Leaders, *Treacy &
   Wiersema*, Basic Books, 2007
3. The Balanced Scorecard, *Kaplan & Norton*, Harvard
   Business Review Press, 1996

Other Books by the Author

BIOTEAMS: High performance teams and virtual groups
based on nature's most successful designs, Ken Thompson,
Meghan-Kiffer Press, 2008

THE NETWORKED ENTERPRISE: Competing for the future
through Virtual Enterprise Networks, Ken Thompson,
Meghan-Kiffer Press, 2008

APPENDICES

Appendix A: The Role and Responsibilities of GBL Facilitators

1. Be an active observer/coach

Decide how you plan to play your role in terms of Topic, Team and Touch and how active you plan to be in each of these (Ignore, Observe or Coach).

Aspect	Ignore	Observe	Coach
Topic			
Team Dynamics			
Touch (Individual Style)			

You should also be looking out for:

- Self-appointed leaders who cause other participants to check out
- Slow Engagers where the simulation is half over before they get started
- Disengaged/Distracted either due to team dynamics or being preoccupied with other things

2. Encourage Teamwork and Evidence-based decision-making

By asking questions and giving feedback to teams about their decision-making, use of all team members and other resources available to them, whether they are considering all the options, not just the obvious, and whether they are working based on evidence and not just hunches or pet likes/hates/preferences/biases.

By enriching participant experience, providing useful information on background and context, but NEVER "inside information," to help a team make a decision. This defeats the purpose, which is to learn, not to win!

3. Steer Team Conversations to maximum value and the learning objectives

The team facilitator's job is also to amplify and enrich high-value conversations and to sensitively shut down low-value conversations. The compass for this is the Learning Objectives, which identify the priority conversation topics.

Experiential and Social Learning opportunities will arise throughout the simulation – often at different times in different teams. The team facilitator needs to help connect these to the learning objectives.

Discourage Low-value conversations:
- What are the detailed rules in the model?
- How do we "game" the simulation?
- How does the exact maths work?
- Why can't the game do X or Y or offer more info on Z?

Encourage High value conversations:
- What Central Dilemmas are we wrestling with?
- What is the Key Business Principle here?
- What would we do in the real world?
- How can we adapt the issues coming up in the simulation to our business?

4. Provide Support to the Key Simulation Stages

- Simulation Familiarisation
- Team Game Planning
- Team End of Round
- Team End of Simulation
- End of Event

See also Appendix S: Team Learning Simulation - Facilitation Checklist

Appendix B: High performance leadership - business game research findings

Over the last 7-8 years I have been running in-house business acumen simulation games with a number of major enterprises who form executive teams for a global enterprise for a three-year period over a single (intensive) day.

A large number of teams, of different levels of seniority, have fully completed the simulation games. Based on observing and analysing performance in these games it seems that there are at least 6 critical differences between top performers and the rest in the areas of leadership and decision-making.

Finding 1: Top Performers avoided the "Presumption of change" trap.

Evidence for Finding 1: Even though the game starts with each team inheriting a business from the previous executive team 95% of the participants showed no curiosity regarding how successful the previous leadership team had been and why!

It is amazing that almost all new leaders focus on what they need to change but not what they need to preserve. What to change is only part of the challenge and for whatever reason (ego, identity, peer pressure...) showing a lack of respect for the previous team's achievements seems to be a good predictor of sub-optimal performance.

Finding 2: Top Performers suspended assumptions, thoroughly reviewed all available instructions/background research and actively sought out any available expert input.

Evidence for Finding 2: Senior teams or functional experts generally did worse in the game than expected and junior teams/non-functional experts generally did better than expected.

As people become more experienced and competent they often become more fixed on their "Golden Rules" ("this always works" or "never do this"). Whilst Golden Rules are generally a good and necessary thing they can also close people down to a fresh examination of the facts available to them. In many cases the evidence that was available would have directly challenged these golden rules if it had been properly and objectively evaluated.

Finding 3: Top Performers rigorously followed the discipline of evidence-based decision-making.

Evidence for Finding 3: 90% of the teams made at least one critical decision which was based purely on hunches or past prejudices rather than any actual evidence.

Evidence-based decision-making is the discipline of supporting every key decision with a reference to one or more sources of written evidence of an objective nature. Ideally this evidence should be representative and quantitative, but it can also be purely anecdotal, provided it can be verified by a third party.

Finding 4: Top Performers were prepared to make painful choices and trade-offs on their priorities where necessary.

Evidence for Finding 4: Team performance was assessed against a balanced scorecard of 5 key indicators covering revenue, profits, market share, customer growth and organisational maturity. In no case did any single team ever perform better than all the other teams on all 5 of these indicators.

For example, in the game to build market share you may need to focus investment on new customers, but to build revenue you may need to focus on existing customers who spend more. In benign market conditions you might not need to make a conscious choice between these two, however, in difficult trading conditions it may simply not be possible to achieve both, and you have to make a choice. Top performing teams always seemed to have a clear hierarchy of priorities - "this first, then this second then this third" - that guided their actions at critical points.

Finding 5: Top Performers displayed "coherence" of strategy and action.

Evidence for Finding 5: Over 85% of the teams accidently took actions that were inconsistent with the strategies they had developed at the start of the game. When this was pointed out they almost always responded that they did not wish to change their strategies.

A key question in determining whether you really have a "strategy" is what you decided NOT to do! If you cannot answer this question, then you probably don't have a strategy and are navigating reactively in response to changing circumstances. This usually leads to "mission drift" and consequent under performance.

Finding 6: Top Performers are open to collaboration, even with "competitors", and are always looking for advantage through "mutual learning alliances".

Evidence for Finding 6: Even though the teams were not explicitly competing against each other, within the game less than 10% of them entered into any dialogue whatsoever with the other teams to explore if they could legitimately help each other or share useful information/experiences.

As well as learning from your colleagues you can also learn from your external partners, customers, suppliers and even your competitors. For example, if you are building a new market it can be an excellent strategy to collaborate with competitors to help build something that will become worth fighting over later. If you operate by the mental model/golden rule that anyone who is not my friend must be my enemy, then you are handicapping your ability to learn faster than your competition, which, in the end, may be fatal for you in your market.

Appendix C: 28 things you can learn from a team-based simulation

Team simulations are excellent "Behavioral observatories" where realistic and habitual behavior quickly shows up in participants and in their teams.

This provides facilitators with a rich range of stimuli which they can both observe and proactively intervene in key leadership performance areas such as the 7 below:

1. Working in Teams
2. Individual Styles
3. Simulation Briefings & Updates
4. Facilitation & Role Plays
5. Balanced Scorecards
6. System Dynamics
7. Experiential Learning

The learning opportunities in each of these areas is broken down into specifics in the diagram below:

A Systematic Guide to Game-Based Learning (GBL) in Organizational Teams

MULTI-DIMENSIONAL MODEL of TEAM-BASED SIMULATION LEARNING

Conflict Resolution	Role Allocation	Group Decision-making	Collaboration and Teamwork	Working in Teams
Collaborative Styles	Support Styles	Team Member Styles	Leadership Styles	Individual Styles
Agility in reacting to unexpected change	Working under time pressure	Developing and executing Strategy	Information Filtering and Analysis	Market Briefings
Presentation Skills	Negotiation Skills	Influencing Skills	Interviewing Skills	Facilitation & Role Plays
Goal and Target Clarification	Soft and Hard Measures	Leading and Lagging Indicators	Understanding Cause and Effect	Balanced Scorecard Theory
Dilemmas and Trade-offs	Feedback Loops and side effects	Systemic Perspective	Mental Models	Systems Dynamics
Rapid Learning Techniques	Golden Rules	Personal Value Chains	Informal & Social Learning	Experiential Learning

**Appendix D: 15 Principles of Business Game Design
for team-based learning**

I develop custom business games for team-based experiential learning workshops, which usually have a significant computer element. This whole area is strewn with pitfalls, good intentions and misconceptions and there is a huge risk that the game becomes too complex or an end in itself, or the graphical aspect of the user interface becomes all-consuming at the expense of the learning.

Therefore, I have been constantly on the lookout for a really good practical set of business game design guidelines (like Disney's Principles of Animation).

The Art of Game Design by Jesse Schell is also a very impressive resource book (with its neat iPhone app) but it deals with games in general, not business team games. Also 100 principles are more than I was looking for!

Unfortunately, I have not yet been able to find just what I was looking, for so in their absence I thought I should try and write my own.

Just to be clear my focus here is on custom games to be played in teams to help the participants improve their understanding of their organizations or businesses. These games may also be designed to help participants observe and change their own behaviors, develop better team skills and improve their ability to manage dilemmas.

I believe Business Games fall into 2 main categories - sharply defined "Skill Games" and broad-based "War Games". The principles I outline here apply to both categories but are probably most relevant to the War Games where you are running a complete business operation rather than a Skill Game where you are developing a couple of specialized skills.

For an introduction to the main ingredients in a business War Game check out 5 things a good Business War Game should help us learn to do better. For a comprehensive set of examples of real live business simulation Games, check out my Portfolio of leadership development and business management games.

So here are my 15 principles - I am sure there are more (and this list may grow to reflect this) but these seem to work for me:

1. CLEAR GOALS - What constitutes good performance? Some degree of ambiguity is OK (just like the real world) but not too much.

2. OPERATIONAL CLARITY - At the most basic level the How, What and When you do things in the game must be crystal clear. At a deeper but equally important level the game must provide the players with the right level of feedback to enable them to formulate mental strategies and game plans. For example, if it is a financial game then it should feedback not just the final numbers (lagging indicators in balanced scorecard terminology) but also the trend indicators (leading indicators). Leading indicators point to how future results will develop unless things are changed and without such feedback players will be effectively "playing cognitively blind" with the only game plan open to them being "try it and see!" This does not lead to the optimum learning experience, which brings me on to my next point.

3. IT'S THE CONVERSATIONS, STUPID - The game should be based around real business issues, dilemmas or trade-offs and not right/wrong answers. The right issues will inspire rich

conversations and give players the opportunity to learn from each other. The most useful games focus on specific company pain-points rather than just generic business challenges.

4. ENGAGING CONTEXT/CONVINCING STORYLINE - The Context and Scene are crucial - this is how you earn the right to the player's time, attention and energy. If you have time you should develop what gamers call a "chaotic story" which is much more engaging than a sequential briefing. Reality is Broken talks about breaking the story into "thousands of pieces like a jigsaw puzzle and diffused across many different media platforms: podcasts and blog posts; videos and online photographs; e-mails and Twitter posts from game characters; even live instant message conversations and face-to-face interactions with characters portrayed by "game masters."

5. RICH OFF-GAME CONVERSATIONS, PROPS, SCENARIOS and INTERVENTIONS - These are essential to capture participant imagination and engagement. Don't try to do it all on the computer. Real people are much more engaging than embedded videos and avatars! There is a very important counter-intuitive principle here: the more you can break the flow between the players and the computer screen the richer the learning experience. So in general resist the temptation to put stuff inside the (computer) game and instead build it outside the game. So, for example, don't put a handy calculator inside the computer game - let the players find, use and fight over a real one!

6. SUPPORTS LEARNING OBJECTIVES - The game should never be seen as an end in itself or positioned to be able to deliver value all by itself. It should be subservient to clearly defined learning objectives.

7. REQUISITE DIFFICULTY - "Requisite" is a great word - it means exactly the right amount of something. Good games are not too easy, but not too hard - demanding but not demoralizing. Also you must allow the players time to take complexity on board incrementally - they should not have to take it all in one go.

8. CLOSURE - It must always be clear exactly where participants are in the game, in relation to the finish line, and that a particular turn/phase has ended. Don't leave them hanging or wondering am I done yet?

9. THE UNEXPECTED - A good game is rational and logical but not totally predictable - it is important to provide changes and the unexpected just like the real world, but don't create total chaos either, or you will just overwhelm and confuse.

10. FUN - It's very important to build in some elements of novelty and lightness - overly "serious games" are little fun and "playfulness" is a great catalyst for learning. Don't underestimate the value of trivia and novelties such as amusing sound effects!

11. FAMILIAR BUSINESS TERMS & CONCEPTS - If people have to learn new and unfamiliar terminology just to run your game then they won't have enough cognitive space or energy left to engage with the REALLY important stuff you designed the game to allow them to explore!

12. NOT A TECHNOLOGY SHOWCASE - The game should use the minimum technology to achieve its objectives - no more/no less.

13. NOT JUST A BIG CALCULATOR - Games which churn out numeric results like an old-fashioned data processing machine

are usually too one-dimensional to engage, and quickly become boring. For example, the results could also depend on how well the participants engage with their stakeholders as well as their algorithmic scores.

14. BIG CLIMAX - The game should work towards a definite climax and be building participant anticipation of this early on so that it ends with a bang and not a whimper!

15. FAIR AND REASONABLE - Whenever the participants are debriefed during and/or after the game on the reasons why they got the results they did, it must make sense in hindsight and not leave them confused or feeling that they were doomed to failure from the very start!

This article was originally published on www.bioteams.com on June 2012

Appendix E: What GBL designers can learn from Aviation Flight Simulation

Even though serious business games and gamification is a white-hot topic it is still relatively early days in the extent to which businesses use simulation in their organizations in a systematic and strategic way.

We can contrast this with the use of simulation in commercial aviation. How many of us would choose to fly with any commercial airline that boasted that it did not use flight simulation to train its pilots and aircrew?

As a qualified private pilot I thought it would be useful to briefly look at the use of simulation in aviation to see if there are any lessons we might draw about the use of simulation in business.

In commercial aviation, flight simulation is used extensively in 3 main areas:

1.   Skills Training
2.   Emergency Procedures
3.   Type Conversion

The main benefits are measured in 3 main dimensions:

A.   Safety
B.   Costs
C.   Environmental Impact

Let's briefly look at each of these areas in turn to see how they might relate to the use of simulation in business:

A Systematic Guide to Game-Based Learning (GBL) in Organizational Teams

1.   Skills Training

Published statistics show that pilot error accounts for 49% of all aviation accidents and a whopping great 83% of all private aircraft accidents. "Pilot error" can be defined as any mistake, oversight, lapse of judgment, or failure to exercise due care by the pilot of an aircraft while it is in operation.

The most common examples of pilot error include:

- Incorrect use of aircraft equipment, such as safety or landing gear
- Errors in navigation, sometimes due to inclement weather
- Miscommunication with air traffic controllers
- Inadequate monitoring of speed, altitude, and other flight parameters
- Failure to manage fuel levels
- Failure to follow procedures in safety checklists

Application to Business: Skills Development

There is a lovely golf quote which over its life has been attributed to three of the all-time greats (Arnold Palmer, Gary Player and Lee Trevino) which suggests "the more I practice the luckier I get." Do you really want your managers and leaders learning their skills as rookies using your live business with no safety net?

Business Simulation can be used for all kinds of skill development for Leaders, Managers and Practitioners. Typical topics that are well served include key management skills such as Change Management or Team Leadership and Executive

Skills such as Commercial Acumen in running a whole
company or business unit.

2.   Practicing Dangerous Manoeuvers

Spin Recovery

Practising dangerous manoeuvers is in itself a very dangerous
thing to do!

In the early days of aviation there was no agreed recovery for a
spin (which is a stall of only one wing). This is a particularly
dangerous flight state as the recovery is counter-intuitive – if
you do the obvious things you will not be able to recover the
aircraft.

Now, once an agreed recovery technique was discovered it
then made its way into the pilot training syllabus, as you would
expect. However, its use in training was controversial as a
significant number of pilots under training (and their
instructors) were killed attempting to recover from
deliberately induced spins. This became such an issue that
eventually some national aviation bodies began to recommend
that spin training should only be attempted in approved flight
simulators.

So the use of flight simulation here has saved many pilots'
lives.

A Systematic Guide to Game-Based Learning (GBL) in Organizational Teams

Application to Business: Company War Games

Most businesses do not encounter dangerous situations until they encounter them for real! Therefore, the first, often ham-fisted, attempt at recovery is often the only attempt the business will get.

Business War Gaming using simulations allows leaders and managers in organizations to be presented with dangerous situations, but in a learning environment which is totally safe and which will not crash the business if they get it wrong.

Realism and customization is key here. To take another aviation example – it is documented that fighter pilots actually scream when they crash their flight simulators under simulated combat conditions, as they have become so immersed in the simulation that it feels like a live mission.

Business War games can easily use senior business executives and realistic paperwork/ briefings to create the sense in the delegates that this is not a drill!

3.   Type Conversion

There are currently four levels of Full Flight Simulator, levels A – D, level D being the highest standard and being eligible for Zero Flight Time (ZFT) training of civil pilots when converting from one airliner type to another.

Flight simulators are now so good that a new captain can make his very first landing in a particular type of jetliner, with revenue passengers on board, i.e., all his previous landings in that type of airliner were in the simulator.

Application to Business: Talent Development

Simulation can be used very effectively to induct new staff and fast-track talent by exposing them to business simulation games, which have been designed using the knowledge of the most high-performing and experienced Subject Matter Experts from the organization (SMEs).

Using this approach, the expert's key rules and judgements can be encoded into a simulation, and if the participants (supported by coaching) make the same judgements they will score well in the simulation, and if they don't they will score badly. This approach delivers effective and fun business acumen transfer to a community of practitioners through a process of self-discovery.

Summary

We can learn very important lessons from aviation about the power of simulation to help organizations develop new skills (Serious Games), practice dangerous business manoeuvers safely (War Games) and develop talent quickly through Subject Matter Expert (SME) Games.

REFERENCES

"The impact of flight simulation in aerospace" Specialist Paper December 2010 by The Royal Aeronautical Society

Appendix F: The 5 major theories of how people "learn": a synopsis

Carlton Reeve has written an excellent series of five articles in **Play with Learning**, which compares and contrasts the 5 main theories of learning (*Behaviorism, Cognitivism, Constructivist, Experientialism and Social Learning*) which underpin personal learning. Carlton also identifies different computer games founded on each theory. I have produced a short synopsis here. It is interesting to note that this synopsis is consistently the most popular article on my blog (www.bioteams.com) each month.

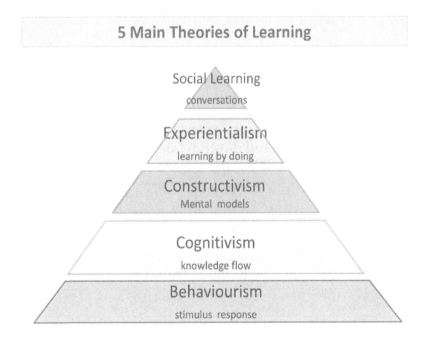

A Systematic Guide to Game-Based Learning (GBL) in Organizational Teams

Over the years, academics have proposed a number of theories to describe and explain the learning process - these can be grouped into five broad categories:

1. Behaviorist
2. Cognitivist
3. Constructivist
4. Experiential
5. Social and contextual

If you are designing a learning intervention you can use this to assess how well the intervention covers "learning fundamentals" identified by each of the theories.

Behaviorism

Key *behaviorist* thinkers including *Thorndike, Pavlov and Skinner* have hypothesized that learning is a change in observable behavior caused by external stimuli in the environment. The key principle of Behaviorism is the reward or punishment of a new behavior, commonly described as the 'carrot and stick' approach to learning.

Cognitivism

Cognitivism replaced *Behaviorism* as the dominant learning paradigm in the 1960s and proposed that learning comes from mental activity such as memory, motivation, thinking and reflection. Cognitivism focuses on the transmission of information from someone who knows (such as an 'expert' as opposed to facilitators) to learners who do not know.

Constructivism

From the *constructivist* perspective, learning is not a stimulus-response phenomenon as described by *Behaviorism*, rather it requires self-regulation and the building of conceptual structures through reflection and abstraction. The learner takes an active role in constructing his own understanding rather than receiving it from someone who knows, learning through observation, processing and interpretation.

Experientialism

One of the key theorists of *experiential learning* is *David Kolb* who developed his experiential model, as opposed to a purer cognitive approach which formally recognized that people learn from experience and described learning as following a cycle of experiential stages (known as the Kolb Cycle - See Appendix N).

Social and Contextual

In the *Social and Contextual* approach, learning does not occur solely within the learner, but in the group and community in which they work. Learning is a shared process which takes place through observing, working together and being part of a larger group, which includes colleagues of varying levels of experience, able to stimulate each other's development.

Carlton Reeve blogs at http://playwithlearning.com/

Appendix G: Behavioral Economics – a very short introduction

Behavioral Economics (BE) is the discipline of explaining why we do what we do. BE attempts to explain why we are so frequently "predictably irrational" in our decision-making and it identifies a number of traps, known in BE as *biases*, which we frequently fall into as individuals or groups.

BE explains why we are systemically and predictably irrational in our economic decisions, and introduces 2 terms "Bounded Rationality" and "Bounded Willpower," as limits to rationality within which we all operate.

A short synopsis of some of the key biases in BE include:

- *Endowment Effect:* tendency to place more value on expected losses than expected gains (also known as Risk Aversion)
- *Status Quo Bias:* tendency to stick with current state of affairs even though we can see clearly better alternatives
- *Framing Bias:* tendency to draw conclusions according to the way something seems as opposed to reality
- *Availability Bias:* tendency to rely on easily available information rather than seeking out harder to obtain but more accurate/relevant info
- *Confirmation Bias:* tendency to prioritize evidence which accords with our pre-existing beliefs
- *Choice Overload:* where we have so many options we don't make any decision
- *Overconfidence Bias*: tendency to rate ourselves more knowledgeable and skilful than we actually are

- *Money Illusion:* tendency to judge prices and interest rates at nominal rates rather than taking into account inflation

One of the most dangerous biases in leadership is the Availability Bias, which manifests itself in two ways:

Firstly, if we are given new information then we automatically assume it is both important and relevant and are likely to give it more weight in our decision-making than the other information we already have.

Secondly, if it is pointed out that we are missing some bit of information, we automatically assume that this information is highly important and urgent and redirect all our energies into trying to find it.

A key skill in leadership is "Filtering" and the Availability Bias, if not recognized and addressed, can seriously hamper this.

This can be very effectively shown in a business game if the teams are first asked to produce their strategy/game plan. Then in the course of the game they are constantly fed with a series of news updates that they must react to.

Many of these updates are about stuff that is outside their control and some of these are pure 'red herrings.'

Lack of filtering skills means a team can get blown off course and become overly reactive to events, rather than sticking to their agreed strategy but in a flexible way.

Appendix H: Business Cases – The Key Calculations

There are a number of different calculations associated with Business Cases [1] including:

Net Benefits: the total benefits <u>less</u> the total costs to achieve those benefits.

Return on Investment (RoI): the ratio of the net benefits to the total costs expressed as a percentage.

Payback (or Breakeven) Period: the time taken for the total benefits gained to become equal to the total costs invested.

Net Present Value (NPV)*: an investment calculation which discounts by an annual rate to take into account the reality that money tomorrow is less valuable than money today. Also known as **Discounted Cash Flow (DCF).**

Internal Rate of Return (IRR)*: is the annual discount rate which would make the NPV equal to zero. Effectively the bank interest you would need on the money to match your project return.

NOTE
If you do need to use NPV and/or IRR, be careful to base your final decision on NPV not IRR. IRR is easier to understand and good for discussion but does not give you absolute value, and does not take into account the number of years for which the return is earned.

A SIMPLE WORKED EXAMPLE

Imagine we invest £100 in Year 0 and get £50 back each year for 3 years.......

Net Benefits = (3* £50) - £100 = £50

Return on Investment (RoI) = 100*£50/£100 = 50%

Payback (or Breakeven) Period = 2 Years

Net Present Value (NPV):
At an annual discount rate of 8%
$PV = 50/ (1.08)^1 + 50/ (1.08)^2 + 50/ (1.08)^3 = £129$
NPV = £129 - £100 = £29

Note the difference between the Net Benefits and the NPV!

Internal Rate of Return (IRR):
The annual discount rate which would make the NPV equal to zero – in this case about 23%
Note the actual calculation requires an IRR calculator (many available free on the web and on calculators)

References

1. Financial Intelligence – A Managers Guide to knowing what the numbers really mean, Harvard Business Press, Berman and Knight, 2006

Chapter 6 (pp 177–196), 'How to calculate (and really understand) Return on Investment' is particularly relevant.

Appendix I: Template Plan for Custom GBL Development

1. INITIAL DISCOVERY
Meetings with Client

2. INITIAL CONCEPT PAPER
Concludes with client Webex/Screenshare Review
Agree Project Sponsor and Subject Matter Expert Roles

3. AGREED CONCEPT
Example screen layout and key objectives
Agree plan with commercials, project team roles, effort and timeline

4. SIM V1
Basic Concept/Main Chain Logic
Concludes with client Screenshare Review/Test

5. SIM V2
Refined V1 plus add client data
Concludes with client Screenshare Review/Test

6. SIM V3
Refined V2 plus add User Interface
Concludes with client Screenshare Review/Test

7. FULL INTERNAL TEST
Detailed test with Project Team and representative end users.
Also acts as initial train-the-trainer session.
Reviews initial version of simulation manual/Training Guide

8. SIM V4
Refined V3 plus Test Feedback
Concludes with client Screenshare Review/Test

9. LIVE PILOT TEST
Full Test with Target Users.
Uses first complete version of simulation manual/training guide. Also acts as second train-the-trainer session.

10. SIM V5
Refined V3 plus Test Feedback
Initial Pilot Run
Also acts as final train-the-trainer session.

The GBL solution should now be ready for rollout into full live deployment supported by a comprehensive and tested pack of participant briefing materials and facilitator notes.

A Systematic Guide to Game-Based Learning (GBL)
in Organizational Teams

Appendix J: Typical Simulation Agenda
(for a half-day session with 3 simulation rounds)

09:00 Introductions, Context Setting, Briefing & Agenda

09:05 Overview/Sim Demo

09:30 Individual Learning Aspirations [Note 1]

09:35 Simulation Familiarization Round

09:50 Team Strategy / Game Plan Round

10:20 Simulation Round 1* (30 mins)

10:50 Team Learning/Sharing [Note 2]

11:05 Simulation Round 2* (25 mins)

11:30 Team Learning/Sharing

11:45 Coffee Break

11.55 Simulation Round 3* (20 mins) [Note 3]

12:15 Final Team Learning/Sharing [Note 4]

12.45 Individual Learning Application

13:00 Ends

Notes

1. Individual Learning Aspirations and Individual Learning Application are the "bread" in the 'I-We-I Sandwich'.
2. Team Learning/Sharing typically asks the teams to reflect on 3 questions and share insights with other groups.
3. Note the reduction in times in each round as game progresses.
4. Final team learning often involves teams preparing a short presentation and ends with the final reveal of the results for all teams.

Appendix K: Blueprint for the design of verifiable simulation models

The secret to designing verifiable, testable and maintainable business simulation models is not to design a single complex "black box" model but rather 4 distinct but interlinked sub-models with a well-defined interface between each of them as shown in the diagram:

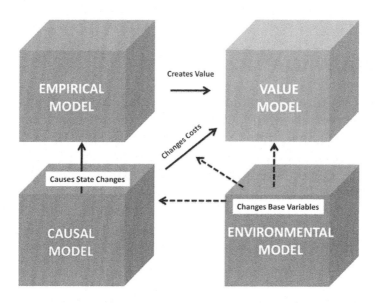

I call the 4 sub-models:

- The Empirical Model
- The Value Model
- The Causal Model
- The Environmental Model

Two of these models are objective and two of them are subjective – let's look at each of them:

A Systematic Guide to Game-Based Learning (GBL) in Organizational Teams

1. THE EMPIRICAL MODEL

This is the underpinning verifiable model of the part of the business under consideration. It should only cover the central entities of the organisation (a.k.a. "the main chain"), such as customers, patients or students and the transitions between their different states. For example, different customer loyalty levels and the transitions between them.

This model should be <u>objective</u> and independently verifiable.

2. THE VALUE MODEL

This captures the value produced, usually but not always, in money terms when key entities (customers, users, orders, staff...) change state in the Empirical Model. For example, how does the monthly average basket size and visit frequency of a "loyal" customer compare with that of an "occasional" customer. The Value model should also cover the cost side of the enterprise so that profit can be calculated. Note that value is not always monetary, for example, non-commercial organisations such as schools or hospitals.

This model should also be <u>objective</u> and independently verifiable.

3. THE CAUSAL MODEL

This covers the main decisions users of the simulation will make and how they relate to each other and the impacts they have on the states in the Empirical Model. Note that the causal model will impact both the revenue and cost side of the Value model. The revenues will be indirectly impacted through the transitions decisions cause in the Empirical model and the costs directly through the costs associated with the resourcing of these decisions.

This model will be <u>subjective</u> but based on real life experience of one or more subject matter experts (SME).

4. THE ENVIRONMENTAL MODEL

This defines the external and internal environments and how they will change during the life of the simulation. External events (shocks or good news) will be outside the simulation players control and have to be reacted to. Internal events can be self-inflicted through poor player decision-making or can be undiscovered surprises like external events.

This model will also be <u>subjective</u> but based on real life experience of one or more subject matter experts (SME).

SUMMARY

If you follow this blueprint, then your simulation models will be easier to change, and probably most important of all, can be verified and calibrated to the satisfaction of the subject matter experts in the host organisations.

Appendix L: 12 Golden Rules of Good Simulation Design

From designing simulations for varying purposes for over 20 years I have accumulated my own little set of "Golden Rules".

There is a real story behind each rule – usually a chastening learning experience!

I share these rules humbly knowing that there are certainly many more rules and not suggesting this list is any way exhaustive!

Rule 1: Einstein's Law: All models are wrong but some are useful.

Rule 2: Machines can be faithfully simulated – sadly, however, organisations, people, culture and social structures are not machines.

Rule 3: Past Behavior Rule: Beware of any simulations which cannot reproduce past behavior (necessary for usefulness but not sufficient).

Rule 4: Some simulations produce forecasts but no simulation predicts the future.

Rule 5: You can have realism or usefulness in models but usually not both (see Rule 1).

Rule 6: In simulation design complexity reduction is the biggest challenge, and abstraction and scope management are the best tools to achieve this.

Rule 7: A good simulation makes visible what is important – a poor simulation makes important what is visible.

Rule 8: Requisite Complexity Rule: every unnecessary equation or variable in a simulation reduces its potential user base by 25% (credit to Corey Peck).

Rule 9: *Clever don't count Rule:* The value of any learning simulation is measured only by the new actionable insights it produces - not by anything else.

Rule 10: *The 7-Year-Old Boy Rule:* No graphical user interface on a simulation can ever compete with the human imagination ("Radio is like TV, only with radio the pictures are better").

Rule 11: *Dilemma-Based Design Rule:* If you want to capture the absolute essence of any function don't model its decisions, model its central dilemmas.

Rule 12: *Occam's Razor Rule:* if you have a choice of two simulation design options, always go with the simplest one.

Appendix M: 3 Types of Social Learning Opportunity

There are 3 different types of learning opportunity, which are available to any individual from a group learning session:

PLANNED LEARNING
I decide I want to learn about 'X' today. I need to be *explicit* about looking for this type of learning.

SHARED LEARNING
A colleague shares their learning about 'Y' and I also appropriate it. I don't need to be *explicit* about looking for this type of learning, but I need to be open and actively listening when others share.

SERENDIPIDOUS LEARNING
I was not expecting to learn about this but it has come up and I will appropriate it. I don't need to be *explicit* about looking for this type of learning, but I need to be open and actively looking for it from wherever it might arise.

Note that these learnings should cover all 3 aspects of the GLB event (Topic-Team-Touch)

Aspect	Planned	Shared	Serend-ipidous
Topic			
Team Dynamics			
Touch (Individual Style)			

It is also interesting to note that all these learnings can also be available to GBL Sponsors, Project Managers and Subject Matter Experts.

For example, in a recent GBL event the sponsors discovered that 40% of the participants did not use critical sections of their monthly operational reports containing key product profitability information!

Appendix N: The Kolb Cycle

One of the most useful frameworks for experiential learning is Kolb's experiential learning cycle. *Experiential Learning* and *Social Learning* (Section 1.5 and Appendix M) are two cornerstones of any team-based GBL event where the objective is learning. Kolb proposes a cycle (see figure below) through which individual learning progresses involving four stages:

1.   Concrete Experience
We experience the world through our senses.
2.   Reflective Observation
 We consciously reflect on what has occurred.
3.   Abstract Conceptualisation
We make sense of what we have experienced by relating the new information to existing meaning structures (mental models) and out of that relationship we create new meaning.
4.   Active Experimentation
We test out the meaning that we have constructed by taking action in the world, which then leads to new experience (then back to stage 1 again).

For more details, please refer to 'The Organisational Learning Cycle – How we can learn The Organisational Learning' by Dixon and published by McGraw-Hill, 1994.

Appendix O: GBL for Core Mgt Skills Devel (Talent)

Team Game-Based Learning can be used to develop skills in individuals which are not related to the 'Topic' of the game. We have already described how 'Team' and 'Touch' skills can be developed, namely:

Team	Touch
Team Setup	Self-appointed Leaders
Team Dynamics	Slow Engagers
Mistakes Teams make under pressure	Disengaged / Distracted
The evolution of teamwork	Other points relating to individual style

In addition, there are at least 7 other **core leadership / management skills** which can be very naturally developed using a team GBL. For the sake of alliteration, I will refer to these 7 skills collectively as '**Talent**':

A Systematic Guide to Game-Based Learning (GBL) in Organizational Teams

Talent#1: Rapid Learning

Central to this skill is learning quickly by learning from, and not repeating, mistakes. Two key practices which support this are *self-reflection* and inviting and being able to listen to honest *feedback* from colleagues at all levels about what you could do better next time.

Further Study

Self-Reflection: A Systematic Guide to Business Acumen (The Agility Dilemma and Mindfulness, pp 100-102)

Receiving Feedback: A Systematic Guide to High Performing Teams (Open Communications, pp 74-75)

Talent#2: Decision-making

To be decisive in taking individual decisions and to rely on evidence based decision-making rather than hunches, instinct and past experience. Where decisions require the input of others to be able to select and utilise the most appropriate group decision-making technique.

Further Study

Evidence-based decision-making: A Systematic Guide to Business Acumen (High Performance Leadership Research, pp 118-119)

Group decision-making techniques: A Systematic Guide to High Performing Teams (Decision-making Practices, pp 80-83)

Talent#3: Strategy (Setting and Changing Direction)

To be able to design effective strategy and plans and when circumstances are challenging to know when to stick with them and when to change them.

Further Study

Strategy, Plans and Change: A Systematic Guide to Business Acumen (The Planning Dilemma, pp 66-74)

Talent#4: Balanced Scorecard (Performance Indicators)

To be able to design effective measurement systems for projects and teams which give an accurate reflection of progress and encourage the best behaviours. To understand the importance of balancing both leading and lagging indicators of success.

Further Study

Measurement and Balanced Scorecards: A Systematic Guide to Business Acumen (The Results Dilemma and Balanced Scorecard, pp 76-84)

Talent#5: Filtering & Analysis (Managing Information)

To be able to assess new information and frequent changes to it to identify that which could be critical from that which is not. To be able to manage information when there is a lot of it and/or when it is constantly changing. To understand what can be controlled and influenced and what cannot (See 'Three Spans Model' in Section 6.5). To understand when your information is incomplete or ambiguous and be able to clarify it ('Naked written goals').

Further Study

Written vs. Spoken Word: A Systematic Guide to Business Acumen (The Planning Dilemma, 'Naked Written Goals' pp 71-72)

Managing Information: A Systematic Guide to Business Acumen (The Agility Dilemma, Managing Information, Commitments and Communications, pp 96-99)

Talent#6: Communications

To be able to provide clear and concise written, digital and verbal communications. To be good at listening to and accurately responding to the written, digital and verbal communications of others. To be able to communicate well with individuals and groups, face-to-face, over the phone or virtually.

Further Study

Virtual Communications: A Systematic Guide to High Performing Teams (Virtual/Phone Meeting Practices, pp 57-59)

Talent#7: Agility (& Resilience)

To be able to react effectively to unexpected changes and to recover quickly from setbacks.

<u>Further Study</u>

Agility & Resilience: A Systematic Guide to Business Acumen (The Planning Dilemma, Agility and Change, pp 92-96)

Appendix P: Team GBL Infographic

The 3 pages in the infographic which follows summarise concisely the 7 Foundations (principles) and the 10 Stars (sequenced steps) of Team Game-Based Learning (TGBL).

Team GBL Infographic (Page 1)

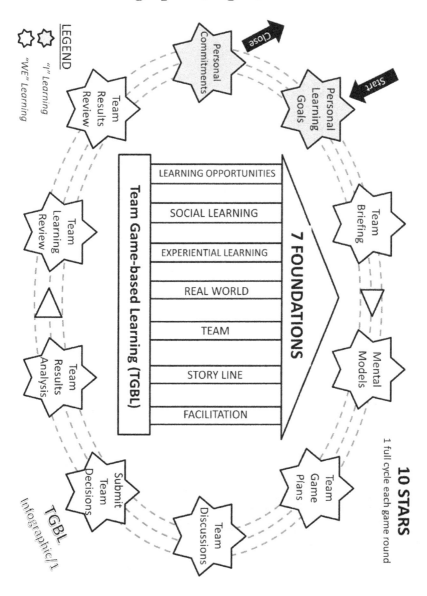

A Systematic Guide to Game-Based Learning (GBL) in Organizational Teams

Team GBL Infographic (Page 2)

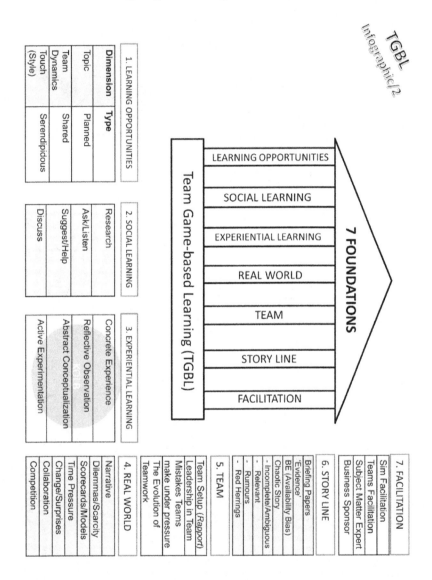

TGBL Infographic/2

Team Game-based Learning (TGBL)

7 FOUNDATIONS

- LEARNING OPPORTUNITIES
- SOCIAL LEARNING
- EXPERIENTIAL LEARNING
- REAL WORLD
- TEAM
- STORY LINE
- FACILITATION

1. LEARNING OPPORTUNITIES

Dimension	Type
Topic	Planned
Team Dynamics	Shared
Touch (Style)	Serendipidous

2. SOCIAL LEARNING

| Research |
| Ask/Listen |
| Suggest/Help |
| Discuss |

3. EXPERIENTIAL LEARNING

KOLB

- Concrete Experience
- Reflective Observation
- Abstract Conceptualization
- Active Experimentation

4. REAL WORLD

- Narrative
- Dilemmas/Scarcity
- Scorecards/Models
- Time Pressure
- Change/Surprises
- Collaboration
- Competition

5. TEAM

- Team Setup (*Rapport*)
- Leadership in Team
- Mistakes Teams make under pressure
- The Evolution of Teamwork

6. STORY LINE

- 'Evidence'
- BE (Availability Bias)
- Chaotic Story
- - Incomplete/Ambiguous
- - Relevant
- - Rumours
- - Red Herrings

Briefing Papers

7. FACILITATION

- Sim Facilitation
- Teams Facilitation
- Subject Matter Expert
- Business Sponsor

A Systematic Guide to Game-Based Learning (GBL) in Organizational Teams

Team GBL Infographic (Page 3)

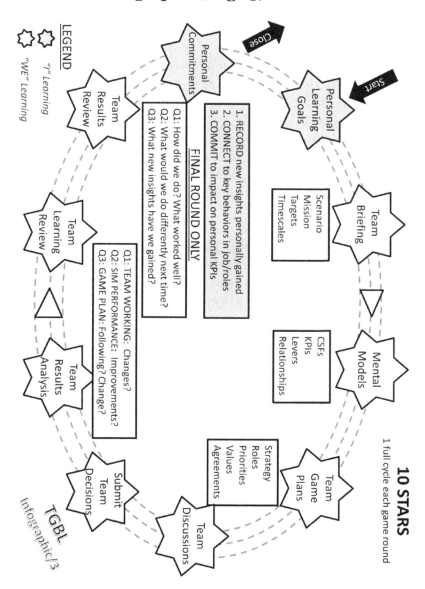

LEGEND

☆ *"I" Learning*

☆ *"WE" Learning*

Close

Start

Personal Commitments

Team Results Review

FINAL ROUND ONLY

1. RECORD new insights personally gained
2. CONNECT to key behaviors in job/roles
3. COMMIT to impact on personal KPIs

Q1: How did we do? What worked well?
Q2: What would we do differently next time?
Q3: What new insights have we gained?

Personal Learning Goals

Scenario
Mission
Targets
Timescales

Team Briefing

Team Learning Review

Q1: TEAM WORKING: Changes?
Q2: SIM PERFORMANCE: Improvements?
Q3: GAME PLAN: Following? Change?

CSFs
KPIs
Levers
Relationships

Mental Models

Team Results Analysis

Strategy
Roles
Priorities
Values
Agreements

Submit Team Decisions

Team Game Plans

Team Discussions

TGBL Infographic|3

10 STARS
1 full cycle each game round

Appendix Q: Review of popular Gamification Techniques

Gamification, the use of game play mechanics for non-game applications, is a very topical area with many enterprises exploring how they might use it to generate new levels of engagement with their staff or customers (current and prospective). In this article, I review some popular gamification approaches/techniques and provide a reading list for further study. I cover 4 key aspects of Gamification: Objectives, Frameworks, Building Blocks and Implementation Risks/Mitigations.

Gamification Objectives

In Charles Coonradt's book, "The Game of Work" [1] written in 1984, he asks himself the big question:
"Why would people pay for the privilege of working harder at their chosen sport or recreational pursuit than they would work at a job where they were being paid?"
Coonradt's answer was to develop five key principles which arguably birthed the whole Gamification concept:

1. Clearly defined goals
2. Better scorekeeping and scorecards
3. More frequent feedback
4. More personal choice of methods
5. Consistent coaching

There are several potential risks and "rabbit holes" around gamification and a good "gamification game plan" is to always keep Coonradt's 5 principles at the centre of your thinking. One other important consideration [2] is that there are generally two inhibitors to any new desired behaviour - volition (motivation) and faculty (skills). If you do not understand the players in the game, then how can you select the right levers?

Gamification Frameworks

In the 2011 book "Game Frame" [2] Aaron Dignan proposes a very useful "Game Frame" on 1-page which identifies the main components involved in designing a behavioural game. Aaron also offers a useful 9-step process covering:

1. Activity
2. Player Profiles
3. Objectives (ultimate)
4. Skills
5. Resistance (aka meaningful complexity)
6. Resources
7. Skill Cycles (and feedback loops)
8. Outcomes (short-term goals)
9. Play-Test-Polish

"Game Frame" is one of the best books I have read on Gamification - under 200 pages but full of useful examples and guidelines. I would recommend it.

Kevin Werbach at Wharton Business School offers a robust 6-step process (A Gamification Design Framework [3]) with the following steps which are well described and supported by a set of videos:

1. Define business objectives
2. Delineate target behaviours
3. Describe your players
4. Devise activity loops
5. Don't forget the fun!
6. Deploy the appropriate tools

A Systematic Guide to Game-Based Learning (GBL)
in Organizational Teams

Both frameworks offer different spins/sequencing on a more
generic 4-step gamification process, i.e.:

1.   Scope out the area and set the business objectives
     for improvement
2.   Define the changes you want to see in player's skills,
     behaviours and attitudes
3.   Profile the players to understand their motivations,
     preferences, interests and barriers
4.   Iteratively design, build and test the behavioural
     game in collaboration with the players

Gamification Building Blocks
A chapter in "Game Frame" [2] is dedicated to exploring (with
good examples) how to employ each of 19 different
"Gamification Building Blocks" in behavioural game design:

Targets -------Puzzles-------Currency--------Points

Competition-------Novelty--------Renewal--------Sensation

Chance-------Levels--------Forced Decisions-------Recognition

Time Pressure-------Social Pressure--------Data--------Status

Scarcity-------Teamwork--------Progress

Badgeville [4], a major US Gamification Technology Vendor,
suggest a similar set of gamification elements as being key
components of their "Behaviour Platform" for supporting
Game Mechanics covering:

1. Points - Assign points for specific high value behaviours and achievements.
2. Achievements - Provide positive reinforcement for high-value user behaviours.
3. Levels - Signify levels of engagement across a company's ecosystem.
4. Missions - Create set of behaviours for users to perform to unlock specific rewards
5. Contests - Create a set of missions, and reward those who finish most quickly or effectively
6. Leaderboards -- Show people know where they stand as relative to their peers.
7. Notifications - Encourage engagement when users perform a desired behaviour
8. Anti-Gaming Mechanics - Set limits on how often a behaviour can be rewarded

One of the risks of these "magic bullet lists" is mechanism-centred design which is addressed in the next section.

Gamification Implementation: Risks and Mitigations
In an excellent June 2012 paper [5] Scott Nicoloson of Syracuse University addresses one of the main criticism of popular models of gamification that they can reduce the internal motivation users have for the activity by replacing internal motivation with external motivation.
A consequence of this is that organizations naively adopting gamification approaches may be creating potential long-term negative impacts further down the line for themselves. Nicholson goes on to identify 5 important design controls to achieve "Meaningful Gamification":

A Systematic Guide to Game-Based Learning (GBL) in Organizational Teams

1.   *Organismic Integration*

If too many external controls are incorporated the user can have negative feelings about the activity. "To avoid negative feelings, the game-based elements of the activity need to be meaningful and rewarding without the need for external rewards".

2.   *Situational Relevance*

Without involving the user, there is no way to know which of the different potential gamification goals are relevant to them. "In a points-based gamification system, the goal of scoring points is less likely to be relevant to a user if the activity that the points measure is not relevant to that user".

3.   *Multiple Paths*

Providing multiple ways to progress within the game allows users to select those which are most meaningful to them. "A scoring system that has no deeper connection to the underlying activity than quantification provides no way for a user to make a meaningful connection to the activity".

4.   *User Defined Goals*

"One of the ways to make gamification experiences more meaningful is to allow players to set their own goals in a way which supports both long and short-term achievements".

5.   *Integration within a User-Centred Design*

"The opposite of meaningful gamification would be meaningless gamification, and at the heart of meaningless gamification is organization-centred design". Another threat to meaningful gamification is mechanism-centred design where game designers see a new or interesting game mechanism and simply decide to build it in instead of designing around the user.

Audrey Crane of DesignMap [6] describes 4-levels of
gamification in a framework which could be useful in guarding
against the risk of mechanism-centred design:

1. Cosmetic: adding game-like visual elements or copy
(usually visual design or copy driven)
2. Accessory: wedging in easy-to-add-on game
elements, such as badges or adjacent products
(usually marketing driven)
3. Integrated: subtler, deeply integrated elements like
% complete (usually interaction design driven)
4. Basis: making the entire offering a game (usually
product driven)

**Criticisms of Gamification from a Learning
Perspective**
Carlton Reeve in an excellent article Behaviourism and Games
[7] (which reviews the 5 major learning theories) describes
how computer games often use Behaviourialist principles in
the way they offer reward or punishment for the player's
behaviour.

"In behaviourist theory, a reward or positive re-inforcer is
anything that increases the frequency of a behaviour.
Conversely, punishment or negative reinforce is something
that decreases the frequency of a behaviour. The strict
(narrative) structure and scheduling of rewards is classic
behaviourism and characterises many games".

Reeve goes on the argue that "some commentators including
the Georgia Institute of Technology professor, Ian Bogost,
argue that gamification is a product of a simplistic
Behaviourist approach to game design". According to Game
designer, Jon Radoff

A Systematic Guide to Game-Based Learning (GBL) in Organizational Teams

"The behaviourist approach to games channels inquiry away from the harder problems of immersion, cooperation and competition that is so important to creating successful game experiences."

Gamification Review: Conclusions

Gamification is an area with high potential rewards but also significant risks if undertaken naively. There are many well-defined gamification frameworks/toolsets available which have been tried and tested to varying degrees.

There is really no good reason to invent another framework and, in fact, this could significantly increase the risk of gamification project failure. The best approach is to adopt one of these existing frameworks or develop a 'mix and match' approach blending the best parts of more than one.

=======================
This article was originally published by Ken Thompson in October 2012 and entitled: Behavioural game design: A Review of popular Gamification Techniques.
=======================

GAMIFICATION READING LIST/REFERENCES

[1] 5 Gamification Rules from the Grandfather of Gamification, Interview with Charles Coonradt, the author of "The Game of Work" in Forbes Magazine Sept 2012
http://www.forbes.com/sites/kenkrogue/2012/09/18/5-gamification-rules-from-the-grandfather-of-gamification/

[2] Game Frame - Using Games as a Strategy for Success
Aaron Dignan, Free Press 2011
http://gameframers.com/

[3] Gamification 7 - A Gamification Design Framework - Kevin Werbach - Wharton Business School
http://irez.me/2012/09/26/gamification-design-framework/

[4] Gamification | Badgeville Website
http://badgeville.com/main/gamification

[5] A User-Centred Theoretical Framework for Meaningful Gamification by Scott Nicoloson Syracuse University June 2012
http://scottnicholson.com/pubs/meaningfulframework.pdf

[6] A Gamification Framework for Interaction Design - Audrey Crane, UX Magazine May 2011
http://uxmag.com/articles/a-gamification-framework-for-interaction-designers

[7] Behaviourism and Games - Carlton Reeve, Play with Learning Jan 2012
http://playwithlearning.com/2012/01/06/behaviourism-and-games/

Appendix R: The Neuroscience & Psychology of GBL

There are two disciplines which underpin all learning –
neuroscience and psychology. In this section, I look at the role
of neuroscience in supporting learning. I then survey current
research about what makes learning effective both
neurologically and psychologically.

Building on this solid foundation I then propose a simple
"Cognitive Framework for Effective GBL." The framework
consists of 12 key principles which can be used as a checklist to
design effective team learning interventions.

The key role of Neurotransmitters in Learning

According to *Andy Brunning* [1], although there are over 100
neuro-transmitters, 8 in particular drive cognitive functions
such as learning, memory and motivation.

"Communication between neurons in the brain is
accomplished by the movement of neuro-transmitting
chemicals across the gap (synapse) between them. These
chemicals are released from the 'terminal' of one neuron, and
accepted by the receptor on the next neuron".

There are two main types of neurotransmitter: excitatory
neurotransmitters which cause neurons to fire and inhibitory
neurotransmitters when prevent neurons firing.

Pete Jenkins explores how "gamification" can stimulate 4
specific neuro-transmitters [2] which in turn promote
beneficial cognitive activities – Dopamine, Serotonin,
Endorphins and Oxytocin:

A Systematic Guide to Game-Based Learning (GBL)
in Organizational Teams

Dopamine

Dopamine is associated with feelings of pleasure, satisfaction and addiction, movement and motivation. The feelings of satisfaction caused by dopamine can become desired, and to satisfy this the person will repeat behaviours that lead to release of dopamine. Games which offer novelty and feedback can stimulate Dopamine.

Serotonin

Serotonin contributes to feelings of well-being and happiness. Low levels of serotonin have been linked to depression, anxiety, and some mental disorders. Exercise and light levels can both have positive effects on the levels of serotonin. Games which offer recognition and praise can stimulate Serotonin.

Endorphins

Endorphins are a range of compounds, the biologically active section of which is shown above, formed from long chains of multiple amino acids. They are released in the brain during exercise, excitement, pain, and sexual activity, and produce a feeling of well-being or even euphoria. Games which offer the achievement of difficult challenges can stimulate Endorphins.

Oxytocin

Oxytocin is believed to be key to how we bond with others and creates strong feelings of contentment and has been shown to create trust in groups and altruism in individuals. Games which promote collaboration can stimulate Oxytocin.

The Goldilocks Effect: Optimum levels of stress for learning

Daniela Kaufer [3] discusses the important question of the level of stimulation required to optimise learning and suggests that "Moderate stress is beneficial for learning, whilst mild and extreme stress are detrimental ..... Stress and performance are related in an "inverted U curve". Stimulation to learn requires a moderate amount of stress (measured in the level of cortisol)".

Cortisol is one of the 3 stress neurotransmitters (along with Adrenaline and Norepinephrine) – how the 3 interact is described in more detail here [4]. Kaufer also interestingly observes that what feels like moderate stress to one person can often feel like low stress or high stress to another individual [3]

Active Learning stimulates many different parts of the Brain

Kaufer also discusses the importance of what she calls "Active learning" where many different areas of the brain are stimulated at the same time. Thus "blending" learning activities which stimulate the lower-level parts of the brain for understanding and remembering along with exercises which promote the higher-levels such creativity, evaluation, analysis, decision-making, association, and motivation can be highly effective for learning.

Structured Repetition is important for Learning

In an article in the Guardian [5] *Ben Martynoga*, a
neuroscientist and science writer, discusses the neurological
benefits of "Spaced Learning". Spaced learning is a teaching
approach where content is intensively taught multiple times
with breaks in between.

Neuroscientists have discovered, originally through non-
human experimentation, that repeated stimuli, with precisely
timed gaps, are one of the most reliable ways to convince
neurons that an event is memory-worthy.

Ben also reinforces Pete Jenkin's assertion that meaningful
rather than trivial challenges produce the best results in
learning by suggesting "learning results in physical changes to
the brain, but dramatic change requires meaningful tasks and
considerable effort".

A Cognitive Framework for Effective GBL

I conclude this section by attempting to extract the main research points into a cognitive framework for effective GBL based around 12 key principles which you can use as a design checklist in terms of whether your GBL is hitting the right learning buttons both neurologically and psychologically.

1. CONTEXTUAL RELEVANCE
Activities which are relevant to the learner's own environment are the most effective for learning. Credibility and context are more important than hyper-realism [7].

2. NOVEL EXPERIENCES
Unusual, fun, experiential and memorable situations stimulate the release of dopamine in our brains which is associated with feelings of pleasure, satisfaction and motivation [2].

3. SERIOUS FUN
Learning is best when learners perceive consequences from the learning activity, so they avoid the mindset – "it's just a game". Involvement of senior business sponsors is an example tactic [9].

4. MODERATE STRESS
There is an optimum level of stress (cortisol) for learning - not too high or low. Example stress factors include changing the environment and the time allowed in rounds [3,7].

5. SPACED LEARNING
Repetition and reinforcement strongly promote retention and retrieval. Multiple short sessions, where the same topics are revisited, are more effective than long sessions [5].

6.   BLENDED LEARNING
Learning spanning lower (e.g. remembering) and higher (e.g. analysis) centres of the brain is very effective. Blend in-game and off-game activities (news updates and role plays) [3].

7.   COLLABORATIVE PLAY
Team-based play and social interaction stimulates the release of oxytocin in our brains which is key to how we bond with others and creates strong feelings of contentment [2].

8.   WORTHY CHALLENGES
Success in difficult tasks releases different endorphins producing feelings of well-being. Competition can enhance sense of achievement provided there are "no losers" [2,5].

9.   FEEDBACK AND REWARDS
Anticipation of feedback and rewards stimulates the release of serotonin in our brains which contributes to feelings of well-being and happiness. Use 'theatre' in recognizing success [2].

10.   TESTING, TESTING!
All forms of self-testing including teaching others are much more effective than simply acquiring knowledge (the "fluency illusion"). Testing before learning is also very effective [8].

11.   PROBLEM SOLVING
Creative problem solving, case studies and scenarios are one of the best ways to learn as they allow us to deepen learning by forcing us to try to apply newly acquired knowledge [8].

12.   FACILITATED REFLECTION
Time for, and help with, reflection is vital. 'Informal learning' - reflecting and discussing our insights - is the best way to learn operational skills. Allow time for reflection and discussion [6].

A Systematic Guide to Game-Based Learning (GBL) in Organizational Teams

THE NEUROSCIENCE AND PSYCHOLOGY OF GAME-BASED LEARNING (GBL): 12 KEY ENABLERS

Infographic by www.dashboardsimulations.com

CONTEXTUAL RELEVANCE
Activities which are relevant to the learner's own environment are the most effective for learning. Credibility and context are more important than hyper-realism. [7]

NOVEL EXPERIENCES
Unusual, fun, experiential and memorable situations stimulate the release of *dopamine* in our brains which is associated with feelings of pleasure, satisfaction and motivation. [2]

SERIOUS FUN
Learning is best when learners perceive consequences from the learning activity so they avoid the mindset – "it's just a game". Involvement of senior business sponsors is an example tactic. [9]

MODERATE STRESS
There is an optimum level of stress (*cortisol*) for learning - not too high or low. Example stress factors include changing the environment and the time allowed in rounds. [3,7]

SPACED LEARNING
Repetition and reinforcement strongly promote retention and retrieval. Multiple short sessions, where the same topics are revisited, are more effective than long sessions. [5]

BLENDED LEARNING
Learning spanning lower (e.g. remembering) and higher (e.g. analysis) centres of the brain are very effective. Blend in-game and off-game activities (briefings, news updates and role plays). [3]

COLLABORATIVE PLAY
Team-based play and social interaction stimulates the release of *oxytocin* in our brains which is key to how we bond with others and creates strong feelings of contentment. [2]

WORTHY CHALLENGES
Succeeding in difficult tasks stimulates the release of different *endorphins* which produce feelings of well-being. Competition can enhance sense of achievement but make sure there are "no losers". [2,5]

FEEDBACK AND REWARDS
Anticipation of feedback and rewards stimulates the release of *serotonin* in our brains which contributes to feelings of well-being and happiness. Use 'theatre' in recognizing success. [2]

TESTING, TESTING!
All forms of self-testing including teaching others are much more effective than simply acquiring knowledge (the "fluency illusion"). Testing before learning is also very effective. [8]

PROBLEM SOLVING
Creative problem solving, case studies and scenarios are one of the best ways to learn as they allow us to deepen learning by forcing us to try to apply newly acquired knowledge. [8]

FACILITATED REFLECTION
Time for, and help with, reflection is vital. 'Informal learning' - reflecting and discussing our insights - is the best way to learn operational skills. Allow time for reflection and discussion. [6]

REFERENCES: 1. "A SIMPLE GUIDE TO NEUROTRANSMITTERS" BY ANDY BRUNNING 2. "INTRODUCTION TO GAMIFICATION FOR CUSTOMER ENGAGEMENT" BY PETE JENKINS 3. "NEUROSCIENCE AND HOW STUDENTS LEARN" BY BEN MARTYNOGA 4. "ADRENALINE, CORTISOL, NOREPINEPHRINE: THE THREE MAJOR STRESS HORMONES EXPLAINED" BY SARAH KLEIN 5. "CAN NEUROSCIENCE SOLVE THE MYSTERY OF HOW STUDENTS LEARN" BY BEN MARTYNOGA. 6. "INFORMAL LEARNING" JAY CROSS, PFEIFFER, 2006 7. MANAGEMENT SIMULATOR AND GAME STUDY, KENWORTHY AND WONG, 2005 8. "HOW WE LEARN" BY BENEDICT CAREY 9. "TAKING SERIOUS GAMES SERIOUSLY IN EDUCATION" BY KRISTEN DICERBO

A Systematic Guide to Game-Based Learning (GBL)
in Organizational Teams

SECTION REFERENCES

1. "A Simple Guide to Neurotransmitters" by Andy Brunning
2. "Introduction to gamification for customer engagement" by Pete Jenkins
3. "Neuroscience and How Students Learn" by Daniela Kaufer
4. "Adrenaline, Cortisol, Norepinephrine: The Three Major Stress Hormones, Explained" by Sarah Klein
5. "Can neuroscience solve the mystery of how students learn?" by Ben Martynoga
6. "Informal Learning", Jay Cross, Pfeiffer, 2006
7. Management Simulator and Game Study, Kenworthy and Wong, 2005
8. "How we learn" by Benedict Carey
9. "Taking Serious Games Seriously in Education" by Kristen Dicerbo

Appendix S: Team Learning Simulation - Facilitation Checklist

BEFORE THE SIMULATION EVENT

1.   Personal Preparation
Play the whole simulation through by yourself. If possible, next do a test run with a couple of other friendly individuals. Keep a notebook of FAQs as similar questions will probably be asked each time by the participants you run the simulation.

2.   Collaboration v Competition
Decide where the simulation event needs to be on the "competition v collaboration" spectrum. Is it totally competitive or totally collaborative or a combination and does it need to change over time? For example, a quite common dynamic is starting competitive and ending collaborative!

3.   Team Sizes
If you have more than 6 players in a team, there is a risk of player disengagement. One way to address this is to have a small leadership team on each simulation team and split the team responsibilities out. Make it clear from the start that it is the team leader's job to get the best out of the team by making sure every individual is fully engaged and employed.

4.   Number of Teams
If you have more than 4 teams then competitiveness can take over, whole group discussions become impractical and your time schedule will be under pressure. One way to address this is to conduct all team reviews just within individual teams or groups of teams and not in "plenary". Also, you may need additional facilitation support!

5. Venue/Rooms

Get the room setup right for the event (usually cabaret style) with all accessories (table numbers, additional large screens, flipcharts, breakout rooms and papers) organised well in advance. Unhelpful room seating (e.g. lecture style) can reduce a team simulation's effectiveness. Breakout rooms can be very helpful. Beware rooms with no windows as they can become over warm and drain energy. Make sure you build in bio-breaks.

6. Agenda

Have all the timings, sequences and paper distribution plans worked out precisely - leaving nothing vague. Make sure you have an agenda and an onscreen visible timer.

7. Technology Requirements

You need a master computer connected to a projector and a computer for each team. All computers need to be connected to internet. Test that the internet is adequate and does not keep logging or timing people out. Talk to somebody technical who knows BEFORE the event.

☐

8. Technology Setup

Get all the technology connected and working well before the session starts and before the delegates arrive. Avoid having to set anything up during a session. If you do have to set something up mid-session, then give the delegates a coffee break while you do it.

9. The facilitation Team

Facilitation is a team job – normally 2-persons - you are a facilitation team and you need to agree roles. Obvious role splits are normally "Presenter (Front) v Teams (Back)" and "Technology v Content". Agree in advance who is the lead facilitator responsible for the success of the event.

10.   Team Setup

Make sure the teams have enough time to get themselves organised before they start playing the sim. It is also important that the participants are given time to ask some questions and think through how they will play the sim before they start. It is each team's responsibility to manage their time - not the facilitators.

DURING THE SIMULATION EVENT

11.   Question Handling

After the initial simulation demonstration don't answer delegate questions unless you a) need to answer and b) are 100% sure of the answer. Otherwise - it's part of the simulation that the players work this out for themselves. But make sure you can answer all the basics (e.g. FAQs) or you may lose the participant's confidence.

12.   Helping Teams

If you need to help a team or an individual, ask them a question - never give them the answer. Remember you need to be perceived as fair and treating all teams equally. However, if a team is stuck they won't be learning do you need to unstick them. Helping a team with technology can be very time consuming – make sure the other facilitator is managing all the other teams if you must provide detailed technology help to a team.

13.   Team Dynamics

Don't just ignore bad team dynamics or difficult individuals or bossy participants or shy participants or people who are disengaged. The best way to address these are by asking teams and participants intelligent questions. For example, "did you all feel you were listened to", "what do you think about that last decision" ....

14. Team Learning

In Simulations people learn most when they are preparing to play and discussing how they did. These sessions need to be actively facilitated and time-managed by you.

☐

15. Avoid the obvious mistakes

The most common 4 mistakes in a team simulation are:

- not getting off to a good start
- leaving the delegates confused after the sim demo
- losing the confidence of the delegates (e.g. technical glitch or poor demo or badly answered question)
- losing track of the time and falling behind schedule and having to rush or leave bits out and as a result leaving participants feeling frustrated.

16. Expect the unexpected

Don't panic. WHEN, not IF, something unexpected happens make it part of the simulation that participants must deal with it (e.g. Internet Failure).

17. Learning Domains

Remember the 3 different potential learning aspects of any team sim and what you are trying to achieve in each one - Topic, Team and Individual.

18. End the Event Well

How will the event end? How will you capture delegate feedback? How will the learning be captured or recorded or communicated? How will you ensure that any delegate learning is translated into personal actions, commitments and behaviours? How will you keep the learning alive after the event?

AFTER THE SIMULATION EVENT

19.   Follow-Up
You need to decide in advance what follow-up is needed to support the learning? Quiz? Documents emailed? Feedback? Follow-up group phone meeting?

20.   Continuous Improvement
Finally schedule a debrief as soon as possible. Review the delegate feedback and your own thoughts as a facilitation team. If you do this the next time you run the simulation, it will be even better!

See also Appendix A: The Role and Responsibilities of GBL Facilitators

INDEX

Your Own Notes (1)

Your Own Notes (2)

A Systematic Guide to Game-Based Learning (GBL) in Organizational Teams

Your Own Notes (3)

A Systematic Guide to Game-Based Learning (GBL) in Organizational Teams

Your Own Notes (4)

A Systematic Guide to Game-Based Learning (GBL) in Organizational Teams

Your Own Notes (5)

Your Own Notes (6)

Made in the USA
Coppell, TX
29 August 2020

34892603R00095